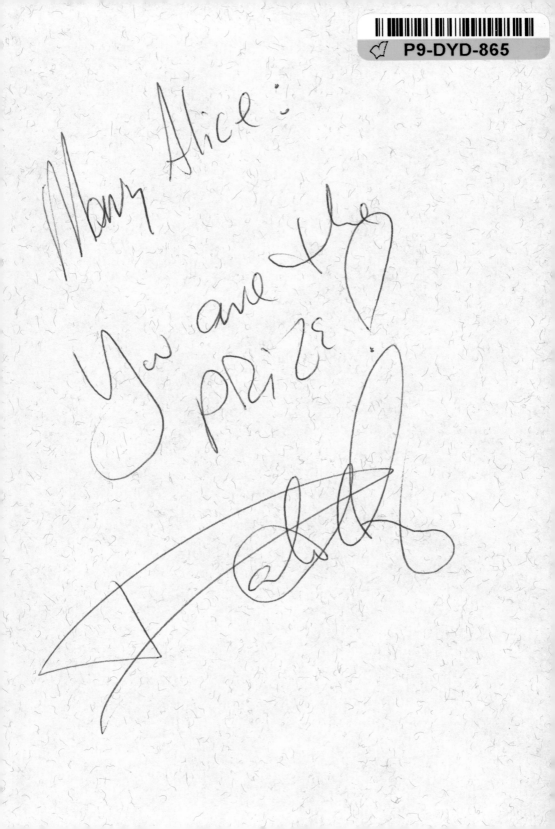

Mary Alice:

You are the
prize!

DALE HENRY

THE
PROVERBIAL
Cracker
Jack
<small>BRAND</small>

How to Get Out of the Box and Become the Prize

Autumn House® Publishing
Hagerstown, MD 21741-1119

The author assumes full responsibility for the accuracy of all facts and quotations as cited in this book.

Unless otherwise noted, all texts are from the *Holy Bible, New International Version*. Copyright © 1973, 1978, 1984, International Bible Society. Used by permission of Zondervan Bible Publishers.

This book was
Edited by Jeannette Johnson
Copyedited by Jan Schleifer and James Cavil
Designed by Trent Truman
Cover photography by Joel D. Springer
Electronic makeup by Shirley M. Bolivar
Typeset: Bembo 12/15

PRINTED IN U.S.A.
06 05 04 03 02   5 4 3 2 1

R&H Cataloging Service
Henry, Dale, 1954-
   The proverbial cracker jack®: how to get out of the box and become the prize.

   1. Success.   I. Title.

                    646.7

ISBN 1-878951-40-8

Dedication

This book is dedicated to the following people who have helped me get out of the box. Each of them has touched my life, and without them this book would not have been possible. They are my prizes!

My Savior and Lord,
JESUS CHRIST

My love, my partner, my wife and child bride,
DEBRA JUNE

My wonderful daughters,
LAUREN MARIE and **DEBORAH LEANNE**

My dad and mom,
ALFRED and **MAEBELL**

My grandfather and grandmother,
FRANK and **JOHNNIE**

My father-in-law and mother-in-law,
SAMUEL and **THELMA FIELD**

My sisters-in-law,
PAM, TAMMY, LAURA, and **CINDY**

To order additional copies of
THE PROVERBIAL CRACKER JACK®,
by
Dale Henry,
call 1-800-794-9409.

Acknowledgment

DEBRA,

my catalyst and my inspiration;

MICHELLE (Broomhilda),

my right and left hand in the office and on the keyboard;

JEANNETTE,

my editor and encourager;

Thanks for making my dream come true.

Contents

Introduction

Each of us reaches a turning point in our lives. For me it was 1972. I was a senior in high school, and I was fed up with the fact that for my entire life my mom and dad had told me what to do. My teachers had told me what to do. As I think back on it, pretty much everyone told me what to do. I wasn't rebellious; I was just tired of being told what to do. So when I graduated from high school, I decided to go out on my own. I was 17 years old, and this is what I did: I joined the military, an organization that was also going to tell me what to do.

I had no way of knowing it then, but it turned out to be the best decision I ever made. There comes a time in your life when you believe your father really doesn't know what he's talking about. But sometime between when I left for San Antonio, Texas, and when I returned home six months later, my father had learned more in that period than I had thought was humanly possible.

Now, you know as well as I do that my dad didn't learn that much, but I certainly did. I can take you back to that June day in 1972 when I physically made the decision to walk into the recruiter's office. I remember meeting Sergeant Grider. I walked up to his desk and said, "I would like to join the Air National Guard." (You might remember that in 1972 we were in the middle of Vietnam.)

He sized me up and said, "Well, we've got a waiting list, son." He pulled out a clipboard that had several sheets attached to it and flipped through them until he came to line 241. "Sign your name here," he said.

I said, "How long is this going to take?"

He shook his head, not looking up, and said, "Oh, no telling. A year, year and a half, maybe."

Being an inexperienced teenager, I just said, "Never mind. I don't have that much time to wait." I had all the time in the world, but I didn't want to wait. I walked to the door, and as I placed my hand on the doorknob I turned and said to Sergeant Grider, "Sir, if I'm 17, do my parents have to sign for me?"

Now he looked up and locked eyes with me. "Son, *are* you 17?"

"Yes, sir."

With a big smile on his face he said, "Oh, then there's another list for you."

That's how I found myself in San Antonio, Texas, two days later going to basic training, hundreds of miles from home and very homesick. If something such as this has ever happened to you, you know what you were homesick for—the comforts of your home, the comforts of not having to think about what to do, the comforts of having your parents, who love you very much, take care of you.

This was my first experience in life in applying the wisdom that my mom, dad, grandmother, and grandfather had taught me throughout my short 17 years. These people weren't telling me what to do—they were guiding me. Unfortunately, at 17 it's a little hard to tell the difference.

The book of Proverbs is made for instruction. No doubt it comes off as being a little preachy, as someone telling you what to do. It's not. It's merely advice from a friend who lived a very long time ago and who also had to leave his mom and dad, his grand-mother and grandfather. And now that he had learned those lessons, he was passing them on to those whom he loved. The problem with advice is that while the giver sees it as beneficial, the receiver sees it as meddling.

For this reason I have chosen to approach the whole idea of Proverbs in a very different way. I want to take you back to your youth. I want you to think about a box of Cracker Jack® popcorn. Remember how, when you opened that box, you could hardly wait to get to that sweet popcorn inside . . . Oh, no, wait! It must have been the peanuts you were after, those sweet peanuts that always set-tled to the bottom of the box . . . Not that either, huh? Well, then it must have been the prize—the best part. We all wanted the prize.

As we get older we want to *be* the prize. Becoming the prize is what this book is all about. I could draw a lot of parallels between a box of Cracker Jack® popcorn and the organization you work for. If you walk through the front door of your place of employment, no doubt you are going to meet people who are all puffed up. They think they're pretty important. I always have a challenge for these people who think they are important. I ask them to go to their of-fice, get a glass of water, stick their finger into it, and then quickly pull it out. If that leaves a hole in the water, they're pretty impor-tant. But if the water fills right back in after the finger is pulled out, then they're pretty much like the rest of us.

Then sometimes you're going to meet people who are not only puffed up, but candy-coated. They'll tell you how important you are, too. And if you're not careful, you'll believe them. And every-body knows that all organizations have at least a couple of nuts.

They're there.

But in every organization, even if there are only two people there, there's also a prize. There's a person who day in and day out takes care of the organization's needs. They're helpful. You might say that their lives are a proverb. Their very existence shows us the way.

That search for the prize in each of us is what this book is all about. It's not meant to be bossy—I have no intention of telling you what to do. But since that June day in 1972 a lot of things have happened in my life, and this book illustrates just a few of them. Hopefully, these 15 short chapters we spend together will give you guidance, laughter, and hope. My true intention is nothing more than a friendly conversation. I would like to tell you that I am an author, but I'm not. I'm a talker—a speaker—and a guy who travels around the country eating other people's food. I am an edu-tainer. My prayer and my desire is that in some small way this book will help you take into consideration some very good advice given hundreds of years ago out of love. May it leave its mark on your heart as you begin your journey of becoming the prize.

PRIORITIZE!

1

Prioritize Your Knowledge

When it comes to God's wisdom,
He has to keep things simple.

Trust in the Lord with all your heart and lean not on your own understanding; in all your ways acknowledge him, and he will make your paths straight.
—PROVERBS 3:5, 6.

Shopping at Wal-Mart is not as much about shopping as it is about going. We all love to go to Wal-Mart. Has anyone in Wal-Mart ever come up to you and said, "Excuse me. Do you know where the batteries are?"

The first thought that comes to mind, of course, is *This person thinks I work at Wal-Mart.* So you immediately respond, "I don't work at Wal-Mart." Now, if that was what you were really thinking, I would be proud of you. But it's not. What you just said has nothing to do with the fact that you do or do not work at Wal-Mart. What you were *really* thinking was *That's not my job.* And if that was your primary thought at the moment you heard that question, again, I would be proud of you. But unfortunately it wasn't.

Let's get down to what you were really thinking. The real thought that was running through your brain was *I will not be your servant.* You see, we have bought into a lie, the lie that to serve someone makes us subservient to them.

Let's go through a short process here of trying to understand what service really is. If you had a mother like mine, chances are she

wiped your runny nose. And probably she wiped your dirty little—
Well, chances are she wiped you. Wouldn't you agree that she
served you better than you have ever been served any other time in
your entire life? She almost died giving you life, and then served you
until the moment you could serve yourself. I think you would agree
that she has served you better than anyone else has ever served you.

I have a question for you. In esteem, where do you hold your
mother—as a servant of low esteem, a lowly person, or as a servant
or person of high esteem? You see, giving someone service immediately places us in a position of higher esteem. So why is it that we
believe that becoming the servant makes us subservient to other
people? If you read a lot of books and if you listen to speakers, you
will no doubt hear things such as this: "To be better, you must do
the following five (or six or seven) things." We live in a society that
tells us we must do more in order to get better. That's not exactly
how it works.

Let's start to think differently as we prioritize wisdom and see
how it can make us the proverbial Cracker Jack® prize. To become
wise, we must do fewer things. And to do fewer things, let's start
with this idea of wisdom in service. There are two things I want you
to stop doing, beginning today, in your quest for wisdom:

1. Vow that you will never look another soul in the face and
say, "Hey, that's not my job."

2. Never leave a situation in which you could have improved
someone's life and say to yourself, "You know what? I wish I had
_____." (You fill in the blank.)

"This is too simple," you say. I don't think so. You see, doing
those two single things will not only suck the life from you, but also
drain you of your wisdom.

Let's do an exercise on serving. This isn't something I want you
to do where somebody might see you—they'll think your butter has
slipped off your biscuit. You will look a little silly, so go off somewhere, maybe into a bathroom. Extend your arms out, shoulder-
high, as though you were reaching for something. Turn your hands

palms up, and time how long you can do this. You're probably going to get bored after two or three minutes and will think, *Maybe I'm a little slow, and I don't get it.*

No, that's not it. The whole point of the exercise is that you *can* do it. The next night, go back to the same bathroom and outstretch your arms again, only this time turn your hands palms down. Here's what's going to happen: After about a minute you'll notice that your hands are a lot heavier than before. Fifteen or 20 seconds later you'll notice that you have to arch your back just to hold your hands in that position. And unless you are physically well developed, you'll find this task to be very difficult after about a minute and 45 seconds.

Even by design, God in His infinite wisdom made us so we could serve and never tire. But when you become a taker, ah! You're going to wear out. Takers and givers have different types of wisdom. That's why the two things I never say—"It's not my job" and "I wish I had"—are so important to understanding God's wisdom. Proverbs teaches us that we must acquire wisdom. Know it. Do it. We must perceive the prudence of wisdom, and use good sense. We must have discretion and the ability to receive and to plot a course of action. Wisdom is placed there for guidance, so that we can hear and understand and move in the direction of the prize.

Scottsdale, Arizona, is a beautiful part of the country, but it can get very hot. The people there like to say, "Ah, but it's a dry heat." Well, so is a blowtorch. I was standing in the lobby of the Camelback Inn after a program, looking at the beautiful surroundings—the mountains, the sky that seems to go on forever. Dressed in a blue jacket, red tie, white shirt, and gray slacks, I probably looked like a hotel employee.

A man came up and tapped me on the shoulder. "Excuse me, sir."

I turned around and exclaimed, "Hey! How are you doing?"

"I'm doing fine," he said, "but I need someone to carry my luggage."

"OK," I said. "Let's go."

I learned two things that day that might be helpful to you. The first was that it's hot in Scottsdale, Arizona. The Camelback Inn isn't designed like a normal hotel, with rooms stacked on top of each other. It consists of little bungalows spread out over a large campus. The bungalow this man occupied was some 250 to 300 yards from the office. The second thing I learned that day was why they call the type of jacket I was wearing a blazer.

We got to the man's bungalow, and he opened the door. Inside were two of the largest pieces of luggage I had ever seen. No rollers, either; they had to be carried. I thought, *Of all the people to help, I had to find a man who sells bricks for a living.* I bent over and picked up his massive luggage and slowly and meticulously started making my way back to the lobby.

In the desert any part of your body that is not covered by clothing when you start to perspire will dry almost immediately. If a trickle of sweat happens to make it all the way to your eye, however, it's a great deal like battery acid.

When we were about halfway back to the lobby, I thought, *Either I'm going to go blind, or I'm going to pass out.* At that moment the man stopped and said, "You wouldn't happen to know the time, would you?"

That was my opportunity to put the bags down. "Certainly, I know the time, sir. It's about 15 minutes before the hour."

"Great. Do you know what time the shuttle's running?"

"Yes indeed," I answered. "The shuttle will be here in about 15 minutes. I know, because I'm on it."

"You, uh—you don't work here? At the Camelback Inn?"

"No, sir."

"Well, why are you carrying my luggage?"

"Because you asked me to."

"Who *are* you?" he asked.

"My name is Dale Henry. I'm a speaker and a trainer. But if you really want to honor me, you would call me a teacher."

After visiting a few minutes, I picked up his luggage and carried it the rest of the way to the lobby. I found out that my new friend works for a company called GTE. (Possibly you've heard of it.) At that time he was executive vice president of sales. During the next year they had three conferences. Who do you think spoke at those three conferences?

Do you think I got those speaking engagements because I was a good porter? because I did something nice for someone? because in his eyes I gained esteem as the servant? No, no, no! You see, what we tend to forget is that God's wisdom enables us to do the right thing.

I was in Miami, Florida, doing a program for 3,500 salespeople. Speaking to 3,500 salespeople is a lot like speaking to 3,500 cocker spaniels—filled with energy but possessing a very short attention span. I was so excited that I could hardly sleep the night before. These people energize me because they are so receptive to learning.

My family had traveled with me on this trip, and my wife, Debra, sensed my excitement. She told me that night that if I didn't go to sleep she was going to make me sleep on the floor, because I was keeping her awake with my tossing and turning. I wasn't excited because of anxiousness. I was excited because I was going to offer these people my thoughts on how to prioritize their lives.

The next morning Debra and our two daughters, LeAnne and Lauren, went down to the pool to catch an early-morning swim. I began getting dressed for my conference. You need to know that my wife dresses me. I don't mean that she travels with me and puts on my clothes, but after 27 years of marriage I pretty much do what- ever I'm told. I reached for my slacks and put them on. Then I put on my shirt and buttoned it. Next I attached my suspenders. As I reached into the suitcase to pull out my tie, I couldn't believe my eyes. My wife had packed a Cat in the Hat tie.

If you are in southern Florida and talk with a Southern accent like mine, and if you come out on stage with the tie that my wife had picked out for me that day, you've got a sign over your head that shouts "Goober!" I didn't want to be a goober. I wanted to say things that would be credible, that these people would hear. I wanted to offer ideas they would understand and would model.

I can't wear this tie, I thought. Then I remembered that downstairs in this beautiful hotel was a little shopping mall, and in that shopping mall was a store called Nick's. So I went downstairs and into that store. I could not believe my eyes! There before me was a rack of size 38 short suits. If you wear a 38 short (which is not very likely), you'll know that most men's stores have one, maybe two, 38 shorts. But here was a *rack* of size 38 shorts in this little store. I eagerly began looking through them.

As I looked at the many textures of fabrics, someone I thought was a salesperson started to hover. I hate it when salespeople hover, so I decided to turn around and speak to him. "Hi. How are you, sir?"

"I'm doing fine," he replied, "but I need someone to mark my slacks."

"Okey-dokey," I offered. "Step this way. Come right over here." As he stepped up on the pedestal I asked, "Do you like plain legs or cuffs?"

"I think I'd like cuffs," he said.

"Good choice. I like cuffs too. Do you like your cuffs a little long?"

"Indeed!" he said.

I started to mark his pants. (I'm not suggesting you go out and ruin somebody's clothes just to serve them. If you don't know what to do, find someone who does.) As I was marking the pants I noticed a man toward the front of the store watching us. No doubt to make sure I was doing it right. I did know what I was doing; I had put myself through college by marking people's pants. So I understood this process.

When I had finished marking the man's slacks, I said, "Sir, be very careful as you step down so that you don't stick yourself with the pins."

He stepped down, looked at his pants, and said, "That's a fine-looking job!"

"Thank you, sir. I take pride in my work."

As soon as he went into the dressing room to take off his slacks, I immediately went back to looking at the 38 shorts. I had one hand up, holding a suit, and was pushing another suit back with the other hand to look at the front of it, when a pair of slacks flopped over my arm. I turned around, surprised.

"I'm ready to check out," he said, placing his credit card in my hand.

"Okey-dokey," I said cheerfully, and walked over to the man who had been watching me mark the slacks. "Excuse me, but could you check out my customer?"

"You betcha," he said, and rang up the sale. When he had finished, he walked back to me and introduced himself. Then he said, "I've got two questions for you. Question one: Do you always mark strange men's slacks? And question two: Who are you?"

"Well, my name's Dale Henry, and I'm a speaker and a trainer. But if you'd like to really honor me, you'd call me a teacher."

We sat in the back of the store for a few minutes in two over-stuffed leather chairs, discussing my philosophy (never say "It's not my job" and "I wish I had . . ."). After a few minutes he looked at me. "Now, Dr. Henry, I know you didn't come in here just to teach me something. I know you probably needed something. What can I do for you?"

I looked down at my Cat in the Hat tie. "Israel, I hate this tie."

He grinned. "So do I."

"I need a tie that says *hootie-hoo!* I need a tie that says *hubba-hubba!* I need a tie that says *oww!*"

"I've got that tie," he said. He walked over to a beautiful display case and ran his eyes back and forth over its contents. This store wasn't J. C. Penney or Wal-Mart. The ties weren't on a little rack that went round and round. I got the feeling he wasn't looking for *a* tie; he was looking for *the* tie. Finally he said, "Ah, here it is, Dr. Henry." He took it out of the display case, and in one smooth movement tied that tie around his finger and held it to my neck. "What do you think about this tie?"

Let's get real simple here, because that's what God's wisdom is— very simple. When we want to learn new information, when we want to get new input into our brains, the first thing we think is *I'll go out and read a book* (perhaps like the one you're reading right now). Unfortunately, the majority of the books out there, especially those in the area of service, leadership, and wisdom, will teach you a number of things—how to act like you care, walk like you care, talk like you care, and, in many ways, even dress like you care. But if you don't really care, you have just wasted your money. The first essential in wisdom is that you have to want to know.

I could see in Israel's eyes that he cared. He knew from experience that this was the tie. I looked him in the eye and said, "More important than what I think about this tie is what *you* think about this tie."

"Dr. Henry," he said, "it's a hootie-hoo tie."

"Then, Israel, you just sold a tie."

What happened next is pretty extraordinary. He sprayed that tie with Scotchgard. He dried the tie with a dryer. Then, gently folding it, he put it into a box. He exercised good sense, because he preserved that tie. "Dr. Henry, stains will fall off that tie," he told me. As he was wrapping the tie up and putting it into the box, I reached in my pocket to get out my credit card.

"Oh, no," he said. "Your money is absolutely no good here." He had already started to internalize the philosophy of never saying "It's not my job" and "I wish I had . . ." He said, "Dr. Henry, I want you to enjoy this tie." He slapped me on the back, and I left the store feeling very, very good. Not because I had just received a new tie, and not because I had received it for nothing. I felt very good because somebody had actually gotten the message.

The girls were just getting back from the swimming pool when I got back to our room. My daughters went to take a shower, and my wife began drying her hair.

"You'd better hurry," she said. "You don't want to be late for your program, hon."

"Oh, there's no need to worry about that," I told her. "I'm going to get there in plenty of time. I would like to wear the tie that's on the bed. Would you mind handing it to me?"

That's when my wife of 27 years said, "Well, well, well! Don't we feel special?"

I didn't have a clue what she was talking about. I thought maybe she was chastising me for not wearing the tie she had picked out. I said, "Honey, what are you talking about?"

"Anybody who just went out and bought themselves a $125 tie has to feel real special." There was more than a little sarcasm in her voice.

"I'll have you know that a man *gave* me that tie!" It was plain she didn't believe me. "Well, that's my story, and I'm sticking to it!" I insisted, and I put on my tie and went down to talk to 3,500 salespeople.

I know when I do my job right. There's a feeling of self-satisfaction. I know I did my job right that day, because those salespeople didn't just stand and applaud. They stood on their chairs. They jumped up on the tables. We had a service revival that day. It's one of those days that "fun" isn't a word that adequately describes what I do. I *love* the opportunity to serve others!

When I got back to my room, I put on some shorts, and my family and I had a wonderful afternoon on the beach. When it got close to evening, we decided to head back to the hotel. Then we decided we needed some ice cream. We made our way down to the mall to enjoy some cool Ben and Jerry's Chunky Monkey. As we walked by Nick's a voice boomed from the back of the store: "Dr. Henry! Wait right there."

It was Israel, and in his hands was a garment bag. When he unzipped it, I saw one of the most beautiful camel hair, golden-colored, brass-buttoned, double-breasted, 38 short sports coats I had ever laid eyes on. It was an absolutely gorgeous jacket!

"What do you think about that jacket, Dr. Henry?"

"That is a hubba-hubba jacket," I said.

He laughed. "I'm glad to hear you say that, because this jacket belongs to you."

Holding my hands up, I protested, "Time out, Israel. You already gave me a $125 tie. I've never owned a $125 tie—"

"Well, Doc, we mark them up, you know," he interrupted.

"That doesn't matter. I can't take this jacket, because for one thing, it's a much too expensive gift for you to be giving me. For another thing, you've already honored me with the tie. Besides, Israel, you could lose your job."

"Oh, no, Dr. Henry," he smiled. "I can't lose my job, because my middle name is Nick. Now, Dr. Henry, if you think you're getting this jacket because you taught an old salesguy never to say 'It's not my job' or 'I wish I had . . . ,' well, you see, you'd be wrong. If you think you're getting this jacket because you taught someone how to fall in love again with serving, you'd be dead wrong.

"You see, Dr. Henry, you're getting this jacket because today, before lunch, you talked to 3,500 salespeople at the convention center next door. And today, after lunch, 750 of those salespeople came into my little store. Today, Dr. Henry, I sold 250 suits. I lost track of sports coats, ties, socks, pants, belts, shoes, and underwear. Today we had the best single day in sales that any of my stores has ever had. As a matter of fact, it exceeded the highest gross sales of any of our stores in our company's history. And I did it by myself.

"To show you the significance in that, Dr. Henry, I have to take you back to this morning. On my way to work I was the most miserable of souls. I was mad. I was upset because my young manager and one of the associates who normally work in this store were sick, and I couldn't get anybody else to take their places. I had to work in my own store. Usually I am very proud to go to work in my store. But I guess you could say that my britches had gotten a little too big. In the past four months I haven't even crossed the threshold of one of my own stores. But today, Dr. Henry, with your help and wisdom, I served."

I might be a goober, and I might occasionally wear a Cat in the Hat tie, but if you were to look in my closet, you'd see a coat hanging there that is one of my most prized possessions.

"I wish I had . . ." "It's not my job." The whole point is to let others see God's wisdom in our lives.

★ ★ ★

I've flown a lot in my time, having spent 22 years in the Air National Guard and having traveled more than 250,000 miles every year to meet speaking appointments. My favorite place on the plane is the back. My whole philosophy for being in the back of the plane is pretty simple. If you've ever seen a plane crash, you know what's always left is that tail section! (I think the tail must be made out of the same stuff as that little black box.)

I also like the back of the plane because you can stand up if you want. You're not in anybody's way, and you can observe people who are getting on the plane. That's where I was standing when I saw a little girl get on the plane. She was so pretty, so full of life, so energetic. Seeing her bounce onto the plane, I remembered that I had won a pink flamingo Beanie Baby from a conference I had attended earlier in the week. As any father knows, bringing home one Beanie Baby to two daughters would be suicide. So I took it out of the overhead bin and held it behind my back. When she was almost next to me, I said, "You are so pretty. Can I give you a prize?"

She turned to her mother, and when her mother nodded, I handed her the Beanie Baby. She grabbed it and held it close. "Oh, Mother, can I have it, please?"

"If he wants you to have it, of course you can," her mother said.

As luck would have it, she sat across the aisle from me. I found out her name was Saundra. I said, "Saundra, I guess you've been over to Orlando."

"Naw."

"You've not been down here to see the old mouse?"

"Naw," she repeated.

I tried again. "To the beach, then. You've been down playing in the ocean?"

"Naw."

"Oh, you must be going to Nashville to hear some country music."

"Naw."

"Maybe to visit some relatives? Do you have relatives in Nashville?" I persisted.

"Naw."

This game wasn't fun anymore. "Well, Saundra, tell me, where are you going?"

"I'm going to Vanderbilt Hospital in Nashville," she said. "I have leukemia. I go every 10 days. I've been going there for the past 10 months, and this is my last visit."

With a big smile I said, "Well, congratulations! I guess you fly almost as much as I do. Do you like flying?"

"Naw."

"Why not?"

"Because I get sick."

During my National Guard experience I flew in practically everything that has two wings. I've been upside down and right side up. I've experienced negative G's and positive G's—and not been sick. My daughter LeAnne loves roller coasters, and I want you to know that I have been on every roller coaster ride on the planet. And *that* doesn't make me sick. There's only one thing that makes me sick: to see somebody else get sick.

"So, Saundra," I said, "when you're on the plane and the plane is bumping, it kind of upsets your little tummy, huh? It makes your tummy woozy?"

"No. I puke."

That was not good. I wanted to clarify. "So, Saundra, every time you get on the plane—*every* time *while* you're on the plane—you get sick?"

"That's right."

I had a speaking appointment in Nashville, and I was wearing the only suit I had with me. One thing I can pretty much guarantee is that people can tell when you get sick. There's an aroma no cologne can mask. I simply couldn't get sick.

As a small boy I had a great fifth-grade teacher. Mrs. Chance knew that I had a great deal of difficulty being still and paying attention. In those days nobody knew what attention deficit hyper-activity disorder (ADHD) was. We just called it being hyper. Mrs. Chance knew she had a hyper little boy who sat in her class, and who was a constant annoyance. I'm pretty sure that single-handedly I kept prayer in Blount County Schools. I believe every teacher who had me in class bowed his or her head every morning and said, "Lord, please let that boy be sick today."

But Mrs. Chance implanted in me a piece of wisdom that she had no way of knowing would absolutely change the way I perceived the world around me. She gave me a shiny penny and said, "Put this penny in your pocket. Whenever you have trouble focusing, whenever you find yourself becoming antsy and wanting to fidget, fiddle with the penny, and it will help you focus."

This particular day on the plane, sitting across from Saundra, I fidgeted with that penny and thought, *I'll turn away from Saundra and look out the window. I'll get some headphones and listen to some music. If I can't see her or hear her, then I won't get sick.* Oh, it was a good plan. I knew exactly what to do. But I couldn't do it. I have to live with myself. I have to get up every morning. I have to look myself in the eye. I have to shave this face. I couldn't possibly turn away from this little girl.

I got an idea as I fiddled with the penny in my hand. I turned to Saundra. "Do you mean that as many times as you've flown, as many times as you've been on an airplane, you've never sat next to someone in the military? You've never sat next to someone who knew how to use the power and the secret of the penny?"

Now her mother leaned forward. "The what?"

"The penny." I think Saundra's mother knew that this was possibly the biggest tale she had ever heard. And indeed it was somewhat of a fabrication, not to mislead but to help her focus, just as Mrs. Chance had helped me all those years before.

I continued. "Oh, Saundra, everybody in the military knows that if you take a shiny new penny like this and place it behind your left ear it causes a chemical reaction between the copper and the bloodstream. It makes the inner ear balance so you won't get sick."

All she heard was "penny," "behind ear," and "you won't get sick." She snagged that penny from my hand and held it behind her ear all the way to Nashville, Tennessee. And she didn't get sick. She didn't even burp. She did beat me, though, at 20 straight games of crazy eights. I don't know how she did it, but I'll tell you what she *did* do—she got into my heart.

At the end of the flight as I stood up to get my bag out of the overhead compartment a small hand touched me on the back. "Here's your penny, Dr. Dale."

"Oh, sweetie, that's not my penny; that's *your* penny. I want you to look at the date—1954. That's my model—the year I was born. So when you look at that penny, maybe you'll think of me, because, sweetheart, I'll never forget you."

And I haven't. I think of her honesty and of that wonderful joy inside my heart that helping Saundra gave me. I'm five feet six, and the day I met Saundra I grew a bit. Oh, not physically, of course, but I grew in knowledge. Perhaps in wisdom. I understood that day what God must feel like when one of His children discovers knowledge.

After watching Saundra leave, I pulled my bag from the overhead compartment. The man who had been sitting next to me said, "I just wanted to tell you how wonderful it was to see what you did for that little girl. I do have one small question, though. I spent 25 years in the Navy as an aviator, and nobody ever told me the secret of the penny."

2

Prioritize Your Value

When it comes to value,
God gives a lot but gets back very little.

A generous man will prosper; he who refreshes others will himself be refreshed.—PROVERBS 11:25.

Most people have a misconception about value. They think their value is that little number on their paycheck. That's not their value—that's only the amount they agreed to receive in exchange for spending a certain number of hours on the job.

Value isn't something you *get*—value is something you *give*.

The majority of us completely miss this simple concept. Most people can remember their first day on the job after finishing college, when they started that lifelong journey to becoming what they always wanted to be. I know I do. I remember getting the call that confirmed I was actually going to be a vocational school teacher. I was so excited! I immediately started working on my first lesson plan. By the first day I had that lesson plan scripted as well as a Broadway play. I had decided every single word I was going to say during that first class. Vocational teachers at that time taught three-hour blocks. So I tweaked my lesson plan until it was exactly three hours long.

On my way to work that first day I stopped for gas. When the attendant gave me my change, she also gave me some trading stamps.

(Trading stamps were a popular buying incentive in those days.) I put those trading stamps in my pocket and got in my car, and off to school I went.

Once I was in the classroom, the first thing I did was reassign the seats in the room. I wanted this to be a wonderful new experience, even though I was starting my job in April, halfway through the curriculum. So I moved the chairs and got everything exactly the way I wanted it. The woodshop teacher had made a wooden lectern for me and had put my name on the front just to make me feel welcome. I spread my lesson plan wide open on the lectern.

Nothing in college had prepared me for having 26 kids come into my room and look at me. I mean *look* at me—right through me. And as they came in and took their seats they focused their eyes on me. All of a sudden that sick feeling of "Oh, man! I'm in charge!" flooded over my body. I thought, *I can get rid of this feeling by getting busy.* I immediately dived into my lesson plan. I started teaching.

Have you ever done something so much fun, so exciting, that 15 minutes seemed like three hours? That's what this first lesson was like to me. I thought, *I cannot believe this! Three hours have flown by, and it seems exactly like 15 minutes!* Unfortunately, that's exactly how long the lesson had lasted—15 minutes.

Two hours and 45 minutes left of the class, and I didn't have a single clue what to do. Then I heard a voice in my head. It was the voice of my advisor and mentor at the University of Tennessee, Gerald LeBoard. LeBoard's voice in my head was saying, "Dale, when you don't know what to do next, well, you just review." I had taught a 15-minute lesson. Not much to review.

My hands started to sweat. My heart started to race. And my skin felt clammy all over. When I get nervous, I put my hands in my pockets. By now my hands were up to my elbows in my pockets. I looked out at the sea of faces and settled on a young man seated three or four rows from the front.

"Can you tell me the meaning of balance in design?" I asked. I was so surprised when he gave me the definition exactly as I had presented it in my lesson—so happy, so gleeful—that I jerked my hands out of my pockets. Immediately 26 pairs of eyes went from my face to my hand, to which a whole sheet of trading stamps was stuck.

Have you ever done something that you thought was stupid at the very moment you did it? This was one of those times for me. I looked at the young man. He looked at me. I walked over to him, ripped off a trading stamp, and stuck it on his forehead. He didn't say a word.

I stepped back and said, "OK, who wants the next question?"

Twenty-six hands reached for the sky. These high school sophomores, juniors, and seniors wanted a stamp on their forehead. I spent two hours and 45 minutes reviewing a 15-minute lesson, and I gave away more than 180 trading stamps.

When the bell rang, I stood at the front of my classroom with a wastebasket in front of me. I expected that these young people were going to walk by, peel off the stamps that were now stuck to their foreheads, their noses, their chins, and their cheeks, and drop them in that wastebasket. But they didn't. Wearing their stamps like red badges of courage, these young folks walked right past me and out into the hall.

I knew the principal often stood at the front of the school, watching the kids go by. That day he was watching my kids like a cow watches a passing train. I thought, *I wonder what else I can do with a four-year degree in education,* because obviously this career was over. I sat down at my desk and started to worry. *He must think I'm some type of moron, giving them trading stamps on their faces. What was I thinking?*

That's when I saw his legs appear at the front of my desk, and looked up. What he said next was only short of a miracle. "Mr. Henry, when we hired you here at the vocational school, we were very pleased. You see, although the other teachers came to us with varied experience from their vocations, you're one of the first teachers we've had here who has a college degree. And Mr. Henry, after 41 years in education, up until this very moment I thought I had seen pretty much everything there was to see. But I had never seen 26 students wearing seven, eight, and nine trading stamps stuck to their head. So I asked the kids, 'What does this mean?' They told me that for every question they answered correctly in class they received a trading stamp. Is that right, Mr. Henry?"

"Yes," I admitted, "it is."

He said, "In all the years of my teaching I do not remember an instance of every child in my class answering seven, eight, or nine questions correctly. That is innovation." He looked at me closely. "Is this something you learned at the University of Tennessee?"

I didn't know what to say, so I babbled while I tried to think of something. "Yes. I think it's called transference. Yes, if I could do an in-service . . . I've got overheads and everything."

Value is not what we receive; value is what we give. I learned this that day as a young teacher. I thought all I needed was more trading stamps, that I could do the same thing again. Unfortunately, as leaders we must do something different every day. And that difference will make us a good value to those we serve.

Sometimes as I'm flying to a destination to speak, I think, *What is it that I can do, what passion can I instill, what message can I deliver, that will add value to people's lives—something that they can use, that will enrich the lives of others?*

A couple years ago I was asked to be the after-dinner speaker at an interdenominational pastors' conference. Every pastor likes to tell a good story or a good joke. So on the plane I wrote a story that I delivered the Friday night of the conference.

On Sunday night I was on a plane going to San Diego. I changed planes at LAX and got on a smaller plane. I chatted for a few minutes with a man sitting next to me. As often happens, the subject turned toward my profession, and we started talking about our lives. He too was a Christian, he told me. He said, "You're a speaker. I'll bet you'd like a good story. Let me tell you one."

The funny thing about this story was that it was the same story I had told two days before in Washington, D.C. This story had already made its way all the way across the country, from one person to another, and then returned to me. It occurred to me that in some small way this story had added value to this man's life.

It's really just a funny story, but I knew that those pastors, as they told it, would actually prove a point. I'd like to tell you that story:

After college three young men decided they didn't want to lose touch with each other, so they decided that each year they would share an adventure vacation. These are vacations in which you go places to do things that are a little bit adventurous but not dangerous.

Twelve years after the tradition had started, these three men decided they would go to Alaska. The area they chose was so remote that they were unable to fly in by airplane, so they chartered a helicopter. The pilot put them down in a small clearing and told them, as they unloaded their equipment, "Now, fellows, this is easy. On the fifth day, at 5:00 I'm coming back. I'm going to give you a flare gun. On the fifth day at 5:00 I would like you to start shooting this flare gun. I'll see the flare from the helicopter and land, and pick you up to take you back home."

They acknowledged these instructions, left the helicopter, and began their adventure. For four days they hunted, fished, and enjoyed the wildness and beauty of all that Alaska had to offer.

On the fifth day two of the guys got up, hunted down their fishing reels and rods, and headed out to go fishing. The third man said, "You know, fellows, we've had such a good time together during these past four days that I would just like to spend a little time by myself in reflection, reading a good book and relaxing by the fire. Since you're going fishing and since I'm going to be here, why don't you give me the flare gun? I'll shoot the flare so the pilot can find us and take us home."

Both men looked at him blankly. "What flare gun?" one asked.

"The flare gun that the pilot gave you for us to shoot on the fifth day."

In disbelief the other two fishermen looked at him and said, "We thought *you* had the flare gun."

The fellow who had decided to stay in camp remained calm, but his two buddies wrung their hands. "That's it! We're going to die!" one said. "No one will ever find us in this wilderness. It's so remote that even the helicopter pilot won't be able to find us without the flare gun!"

"Guys, don't worry about it, because everything is going to be OK," their friend soothed.

"You really think so?" they said.

"Yes indeed. I guarantee it."

That seemed to calm them down. They built a big smoking fire, but although the fire burned almost continuously for three days, no helicopter came. They decided they would start walking south. *If we start walking south,* they reasoned, *at least we're doing something. We're moving.*

And for three days they didn't see a single solitary living soul. And each day, with growing intensity, these two pessimists would start to worry and whine. Each time their friend would console, they became a little more afraid.

Finally, after several more days of absolutely no contact from any other human being, the two men cornered their friend. "Look," they said, "if there's something you know, if there's a piece of information that would just plant hope in us, would somehow instill in us the faith that we'll be found, please tell us, won't you?"

Reluctantly their friend replied, "Well, it's a personal kind of thing, but if it will make you feel any better, I'll tell you. Do you remember the first time we went on one of these vacations?"

"Yes, of course we remember," they said. "We went down the Colorado River through the Grand Canyon. Oh, man, that's the trip you fell out of the raft. We thought we'd lost you. We thought you had drowned."

"So did I. And somehow a hand reached down into that river and pulled me up into the rubber raft, and I have to tell you, guys, it was a religious experience. As soon as I got home I renewed my conviction to be a stronger Christian. However, on that night—and on every night that followed it—I had a dream. And that dream was that God wanted me to tithe 25 percent of my salary."

"Wow!" his friends breathed. "That seems awfully excessive."

"Oh, *you* think it seems excessive! I fought it! And every night the dream came back. As a matter of fact, if I would wake up in the middle of the night, I would have the dream again. After four months I decided to give in, and started tithing 25 percent of my salary. At the time I was making $60,000 a year. The next year I made $120,000. The year after that I made $240,000. And every year for the past 12 years my salary has doubled. Last year I made more than $12 million."

With a great deal of concern and a puzzled look on their faces his friends asked, "What does that have to do with us being here in Alaska, with being rescued?"

"Don't worry," smiled their friend. "My pastor will find me!"

You see, love and faithfulness really don't have anything to do with money but a great deal to do with the way we look at value. Prosperity really has nothing to do with how much we give God, but rather how much God wants to give us. As our tithe, that amount of money that we return to God, God asks only for 10 percent back of the 100 percent that He gives us every single day. That's value!

There's no way that you can prioritize without first understanding that to give a priority to something places it first in your life. I often challenge people to pick up their checkbook and their day planner and look inside. If I asked, "What is your priority in life?" you would have an answer. But I would challenge you to look in your day planner and ask yourself, "Where do I spend the majority of my time?" If God is not your priority, then your priority is all out of shape.

Look in your checkbook. Where do you spend the majority of your money? Your money also shows your priority in life. God expects us to be of value not just to others but also to Him. He wants our lives to reflect what our priorities in life actually are. As Christians our priority should be to add value both to others and to our Master, Jesus.

When we think of love and faithfulness, we need to understand the importance that Scripture reading—Bible study—plays in a Christian's life. It helps us set our priorities. The way we show love and faithfulness to God is through our actions. It's quite easy to pretend to do something, to be a good Christian around other good Christians. But as long as we are in a vertical position, people watch us. They watch what we do. They watch what we say. And we cannot show love and faithfulness without being the same way all the time. We will be judged by what we do, not by what we say we're going to do.

When I was a young teacher, I remember getting a letter from the state of Tennessee that said something like this: "The Governor of the State of Tennessee would like to announce the career ladder." The career ladder was a three-step plan. Once you had enough time and experience, you could actually make $7,000 by reaching the top rung of the career ladder. That would double a teacher's salary.

I got excited! Who wouldn't? The first thing I had to do was take a test. No sweat. Teachers are good at tests—we give them, so why can't we take them? So I took the test, and I passed.

The next step of the career ladder was to put together a portfolio. Whoa! I had no clue what that was. But I asked around and found out that a portfolio is really a brag book about what you've done. It's also a book about what you'd like to do, a book of goals, lesson plans, and achievements that you'd like to have or make happen. It's a book about value. I put together a portfolio. This portfolio was massive! You would have gotten a hernia just from carrying this thing across the room. I sent it to Nashville, and the folks in Nashville said, "Congratulations! You have now made the second rung of the career ladder."

Now I was in for my next big surprise. Yes, surprise. That's a word often used on your birthday when you receive a present. But the surprise I was going to receive wasn't that kind of surprise. The requirements for the third rung of the ladder went like this: "Next you're going to be evaluated by five of your peers. The set of criteria that you will be evaluated by is a surprise."

I don't think that's a surprise; that's some kind of "Gotcha!" Nevertheless, I set about the task of trying to figure out by what criteria I would be evaluated. I thought, *What a waste of time!* I called around and found other people who had gone through their surprise, and I got a copy of that criteria. I went down the checklist, checking it off. "Oh, I do that . . . I do that . . . I do that . . . Uh-oh! I don't do that. As a matter of fact, I don't think I've ever done *that!*"

You see, "what" they wanted was for my kids to raise their hands in class after every question. From my experience of teaching in high school I had learned that high school students do not like to raise their hands—unless you have trading stamps. I also think I told you I taught vocational high school. *They* definitely don't like to raise their hands. But I had to have their cooperation. I had to be able to get them to show me some outward motion that they knew something.

So in class the next day I said, "Folks, I need you on my team. I need you to help me accomplish a goal. Here's my goal: As you well know, I teach a certain way, and I'm going to be evaluated over the next several weeks. I'm not going to do anything differently, but there is one thing these evaluators will be looking for. They are expecting me to have you raise your hands. You know I don't make you do that. Instead, I get out my grade book every day and ask each of you specifically.

"So I'm going to go through the lesson as I always do; however, at the end of the lesson I'm going to say, 'Now, I'm going to ask some questions.' When you hear the word 'questions,' that's your cue, and here's what I want you to do: I want everybody in the room to raise their hand—the right hand if you know the answer, the left hand if you don't."

Well, we practiced, and we got pretty good at it. When the evaluator came to my room, we were ready. I taught my lesson as I always did, right up to that part of the class when I said, "Now, I have some questions." They didn't let me down. When I asked a question, there were right hands raised, and there were left hands raised. I thought, *How good this is!*

They all were doing an action. Some of them were showing by their action that they knew what they were doing. And some, by raising their left hand, were saying, "I don't have a clue." That wasn't a bad thing. At least they were doing something. Most of us don't do anything. Instead of raising our right hand or our left hand, we merely put our heads down because we think Christians should be meek. God does not call us to be meek! God calls us to action! God calls us to value!

I got so excited seeing my students raise their hands that for a moment I don't know what happened. A lapse of memory, perhaps; a misjudgment. But I looked to the back left-hand corner of my room, and there was Jim Johnson, holding up his right hand. Jim wasn't an outstanding student. As a matter of fact, I don't recall him answering many questions in the two years he had been in my class. But I got so excited that he had held up his right hand that I called out, "Jim, tell the class! Tell them the answer, my friend."

Whereupon he said, "Uh-oh, wrong hand."

As we go through life we need to make sure that we're raising the right hand, the hand that says, "I want to do some things. I want to take my prosperity, what's happening to me, and transfer it—not give it, but transfer it—to others. I want to give those people around me love and faithfulness. I want them to understand the importance of supplying the needs of other people.

I try to add value. I believe that people watch me. And I want them to watch me. I want so desperately for them to see Jesus in me that I try my best to be upbeat at every moment. When I slip, when something makes me center on myself, I know that people will not be able to see Jesus in my life.

Almost everybody has had someone walk up to them and say, "Hey! How are you?" And the answer usually comes back, "I'm fine." Don't do that! That is nothing but ritual. What does "fine" mean? Nothing! I want to be an example. I want to "clean people up," as I call it.

This ability to clean people up came from my grandfather. My grandfather had a rather large toolshed. Occasionally I would go over to borrow something. Coming back with a dirty hoe one day because it had rained the night before, I started to go into the toolshed with this hoe caked with dirt and mud.

With his arm across the toolshed door my grandfather asked me, "Where do you think you're going, son?"

"To put this tool up again, Papaw."

He said, "I don't think so. You see, son, you have the opportunity as you live your life to do one simple thing that can make a difference in others' lives. Every time somebody gives you something to use that belongs to them, clean it up before you give it back."

I have long since stopped using tools out of my grandfather's shed. But every day I get the opportunity to use someone's time when I meet and greet them. And since they have given me a gift—a gift of themselves and a gift of their time, a gift that I cannot replace—I try to "clean" those gifts up. So whenever I get the opportunity, I try my best to get people to slip out of the ritual and slip into the here and now. I try to show them how wonderful it is to walk and breathe and see and hear the blessings that God has given us.

When a restaurant host asks, "Will that be smoking or non-smoking?" I usually say, "Well, you know, how about the spitting section?" She laughs.

As I board a plane the flight attendant often stands at the door and says, "Hello! How are you? Hello! How are you?" Out of habit 10 people in front of you and 10 people behind you will repeat the same reply. But when I walk in, I answer, "You know, if I were a dog, I'd be wagging my tail!" They usually laugh, and I continue, "Do you really want to make my day?" When they say yes (because they want to be helpful), I say, "Then you can bring me that little black box."

"Why on earth would you want that little black box?" they wonder.

"Because they *always* find that little black box. And if they always find that little black box, they'll find me!"

It cleans them up, changes their point of view. I have no control over the quality of people around me other than to clean them up and change that quality. Maybe you're saying, "Dale, what does that have to do with having Jesus in you?" Just this: People will not listen to you until you give them a reason. I have always had trouble witnessing to other people. But God has given me the gift to stand in front of others, secular audiences, and talk about His love. And no matter how it comes out, people come to me after the program, embracing me, hugging me, and say, "Oh, how wonderful to have a Christian speaker." Through my actions they can see Jesus in me.

Value is something we add to those around us. The cleaning-up process that we do through changing our lives and changing our leadership styles causes those people around us to see the value. I know of no other story that illustrates this better than what I call the value story.

I was sitting at home one day when I received a phone call that went something like this:

"Hi! My name is Jim Wilson, and I'm with MCI."

Immediately I responded, "Mr. Wilson, I enjoy my long-distance service."

He started to laugh and said, "No, Dr. Henry, I don't want to change your long-distance service—I want you to come and do a program for me. We're having a program in Nashville, Tennessee, and I would like you to come and present at that conference."

I said, "I would love to, Mr. Wilson. Would you mind telling me the dates of the program?" When he did, I said, "Look, I can put you on hold, or I can call you back."

He said, "I don't mind being on hold." So I put him on hold and called my office to check my calendar. My secretary said, "Oh, Dale, that date has a line through it, and it's a yellow line." That meant that I had committed myself to doing something else that day. It just so happened that I was to go camping.

So I reconnected with Mr. Wilson and reported, "Mr. Wilson, I'm so sorry, but I have a commitment that day."

"You're speaking for someone else?"

"No, Mr. Wilson, I told my family that I'm going camping."

"No problem," he said. "I only want you to speak from 9:00 to 10:00."

I said, "Mr. Wilson, I understand what you're wanting, but you see, I live in another time zone from Nashville. It's an hour later at home, and if I did your program from 9:00 to 10:00 . . . Let me be totally honest with you. After speaking, I can't just leave at 10:00. I like to hang around and talk with people and exchange ideas and really get to know the audience. You see, just standing up for the hour and doing the presentation isn't the cause for my passion. The passion happens afterward. It's that interaction of drawing those people of quality around me. That's what I love to do."

"Well, Dr. Henry, you could probably still do that and get home in time to go camping," he argued.

"I don't think so, Mr. Wilson," I countered. "You see, if I do your program, then I probably won't leave until 12:00. That's 1:00 at my home. Add the two-hour drive, and it will be 3:00. By the time I change my clothes, it will be 4:00, and by the time we get up to the mountains, it's going to be dark. I just don't believe my family would enjoy that. I gave them my word. I can't write a check with my mouth that I'm not willing to cash with my actions."

He was quiet for a moment, then said, "You know, Dr. Henry, I understand very well what you're saying. You see, I have a family too, and I understand the importance of family. But let's look at it this way: What if you bring your family and spend three days in Nashville? Dr. Henry, have you ever stayed in that big suite at the Opryland Hotel? The big one, Dr. Henry, that's right over the dancing water—the one where the guy plays the harp."

"Oh, that's a very nice suite," I replied. "We saw that suite once when I was there doing a nursing conference. It is indeed lovely."

"Dr. Henry, we're going to put you in that suite all three nights."

I said, "You know, Mr. Wilson, I travel around the country, and one of the things I talk about is value and how we add value to the lives of others. I've got to tell you something: You're pretty good, but I have to say no. You see, I've committed to my family."

He sighed. "Well, it's important to keep that commitment, Dr. Henry. And I understand how important that is for you. But do you like the blues?"

"Well, yeah, I like the blues, Mr. Wilson, but I don't understand what that's got to do with me and my family."

"We're going on a blues cruise."

"We like the blues very much, and we would enjoy that a lot."

"You see, you're going to be at the front table. You're going to be there with your family, enjoying the blues."

"Well, my family likes the blues," I said.

"See?" he pointed out. "That would add value."

"No, you don't understand," I objected. "I'm going to take my family camping."

"I understand. Say, Dr. Henry, do you like Reba McEntire?"

"Oh, yeah! I love Reba McEntire."

"Well, you know what? We're going to have a concert at our conference. Reba McEntire is going to do a program for us. You are going to be on the front row of that program. You're going to get to go backstage and meet her and have a reception with her. Your family would enjoy that, wouldn't they, Dr. Henry?"

I had to agree. "They would enjoy it very much. And I need to correct something, Mr. Wilson. I told you that you were pretty good at value. I was wrong. You're *extremely* good! But I've still got to say no."

"I understand."

"No, I don't believe you do," I said. "In my household it goes like this: If mama ain't happy, ain't nobody happy! And I have told my wife that we're going camping."

He laughed. "Tell me about your wife, Dr. Henry."

"Well, Debra used to be a teacher—"

"No, no, no, no, Dr. Henry, tell me what she likes to do."

"Oh. My wife and my girls love to ride horses."

He gasped. "You're not going to believe this! The vice president of our company owns a quarter horse ranch in Goodlettsville, Tennessee. Let me just lay the whole package out for you: You're going to come and stay in the beautiful suite—the huge suite over the dancing water—and you're going to hear the harp being played at the Opryland Hotel.

"And you're going to go out on the *General Jackson* for a blues cruise. And after the blues cruise you're going to get up the next morning, do an hour's presentation for us, Dr. Henry, just an hour—from 9:00 to 10:00—and we're going to pay your fee.

"Then later on that afternoon you're going to go to a concert given by Reba McEntire. You will be sitting on the front row. And you're going to have backstage passes, and you'll get to go to a reception where you'll meet her.

"And then, Dr. Henry, the next morning you're going to get up and go to this wonderful quarter horse ranch in Goodlettsville, Tennessee.

"Dr. Henry, we just want you for an hour. Won't you come and do your program for us? We'll pay your fee."

I didn't say anything. It wasn't doing any good to answer him, because he was very determined. Finally I said, "Mr. Wilson, please try to understand. Value to me is taking care of my family and taking care of the things they want to do. I want to do your program because I love being in front of people. I love the opportunity to speak! But getting what *I* want won't be value to my family."

He said, "I want to call you tomorrow, Dr. Henry."

"Mr. Wilson, you can call me all you want to, and I'd love to do your program. Maybe I can do it next year."

"I'll call you tomorrow."

I said OK and hung up the phone. I looked over, and there on the second step from the top of the stairs leading into my office was my wife, hands on her hips.

"Did I hear you talking about that weekend we're going camping?" she demanded.

"Yes, ma'am, you did." (I always find it's best to say "Yes, ma'am" when you think you're in trouble.) "But if you had listened very carefully—which I know you probably did—you would have also heard me tell him, "No, no, no. No, no, no."

The hands went down, and she walked over. She embraced me (I love it when my wife embraces me) and said this: "Honey, we know you love what you do. And we know it gives you a great deal of pleasure, because you are impassioned to help others. But we love you, and we love to be with you. And we so crave you when you are not with us. I want you to know that what you do for our family is to give of yourself. And we love it when you're with us! Thank you for giving yourself to us."

Well, that kind of made me feel guilty, so I said, "Honey, that was one of the nicest things you've ever said to me."

She said, "I intended it to be."

"Since you've been honest with me, I feel it's only fair that I should tell you what Mr. Wilson wanted to do. He wanted to give us that suite at the Opryland Hotel—you know, the big one over the dancing water."

And Debra said, "Oh! That room is so pretty! The one we saw at the nursing conference!"

"That's the one. He was going to give us that room for three nights."

"That would be so beautiful!" she said.

"I know, but we're going camping," I reminded her. "And he was going to let us go on a blues cruise on the *General Jackson* and sit on the front row. Then I was going to get up the next morning and do their program from 9:00 to 10:00, for which he was going to pay me the full fee. Then he was going to let us go to Reba McEntire's concert and have backstage passes. And the next morning he was going to let us go to Goodlettsville, Tennessee, where you and the girls were going to get to ride horses at a beautiful quarter horse ranch."

"Did you say Goodlettsville, Tennessee?"

"Yes, I did."

"Wait right here," she said and ran downstairs and got a copy of *Southern Living* magazine. She came back up and opened it to a certain page. "Is this the quarter horse ranch you're talking about?"

"Yes, that's it. That's the one he mentioned."

She said, "Please, please call him back!"

Why the change of heart? Because, you see, something that gave me so much pleasure was also going to give my family pleasure. It was going to be value to them. I would get to speak (something I'm very passionate about). They were going to get to have fun (something they love to do). But they were going to get to do it *with* me. The whole reason for going camping was to be *with* me. We were going to be together. That's value to my family, the time we share.

Lots of people think prosperity is value. They think that a proper attitude toward money means the ability to acquire it. It does not. The proper attitude about money is giving to God that which belongs to God. Even though He enables us to keep 90 percent of what we make, we see it as "my" money. It's not your money. God blesses you with money so that you can give back value to others:

★ love and faithfulness, the importance of supplying others' needs, and studying the Bible to give you guidance in your life

★ loving your neighbors, surrounding yourself with good folks, and avoiding bad company

★ keeping your paths straight

★ disciplining your body not only to act in a right way but to show Jesus through your life

God wants you to trust Him. Even though He can't trust us, we can trust Him. He wants us to lay aside our selves and put on Jesus so that people can see Jesus in our lives. That is the least and the best and the most wonderful thing we can do.

When it comes to value, God gives a lot but gets very little. Because of His love for us, because of His heart, He wants us to live fearlessly, trusting Him and being a good disciple, disciplining ourselves to be closer to Him. So when we turn from that thing that is important to us, when we turn from just having people around us to surrounding ourselves with quality people, that is how we build value.

Each of us is a turtle on a fence post. If any of you know anything about turtles, you know they can't climb. If they're on a fence post, somebody had to put them there. In our goal-setting experiences in life, we think we can set ourselves up, but we're not good climbers either. If we have made it to the top of the fence post, it is because an outstanding individual has reached down and helped us get up there.

God wants to do that for you too. God is the ultimate mentor. And the life of Jesus is the example we strive for, that of constantly serving others, turning them into disciples as well.

3

Prioritize Responsiveness and Integrity

So if the plane were going down, what would you do?

A patient man has great understanding, but a quick-tempered man displays folly.—PROVERBS 14:29.

The bamboo tree is planted in much the same way as a country boy like me would plant watermelon. A mound is formed, and a single seed is inserted into the mound. But the similarities stop there. For a year the soil around the bamboo tree is cultivated and watered constantly. And nothing happens. The second year the soil is cultivated and watered. And nothing happens. The third year, as in the previous two, the soil is cultivated and watered. Then, in a six-week period, the bamboo tree grows 90 feet.

The question you have to be asking yourself is When did the bamboo tree start to grow? Of course it began growing the second the seed germinated. It probably sent down roots and began building a system that would support the huge tree it was to become.

Responsiveness and integrity grow in our lives in the same way. We send down roots—a device that helps us support our decision-making skills. And in that root system—in the main part, the part of strength—live responsiveness and integrity.

One winter in Greeneville, Tennessee, when I was a college dean, we had an uncommonly deep, wet snowfall unlike any snow we had had before. I knew immediately that students soon would be calling, wanting to know if we were going to be having classes. After conferring with one of my staff members, who called the television and radio stations, we canceled classes.

Since I was freed from regular duties and nobody else was in the office, I thought I would go work out. Working out was not something I did all the time. Don't get me wrong; I love to exercise. Running is my favorite form of exercise. But on this particular day I decided I would go work out in the gym. If you know anything about a college campus, you will understand my reasoning. Nobody, especially students, is going to get up early in the morning unless there's school, and, of course, we had canceled classes.

I made my way to the back of the gym where smaller weights were located in a rack. I picked up a couple of 15- or 20-pound weights and tried to get my cardiovascular system to kick in. I had started to build up a pretty good sweat when the door to the gym opened, and in stepped the center of the football team. We're talking about a young man here, who had no neck—just a body and a head. He immediately went to the weight bench.

Now, I don't know that much about free weights, but I could tell within the few minutes that he was there lining up the weights that he had roughly the equivalent of the front end of my automobile assembled on the bar at the weight bench. Crawling underneath, he positioned himself, then shouted at me from the middle of the gym.

"Dr. Henry, I need someone to spot me!"

It's important to know that I weigh 145 pounds. This was possibly the fifteenth or twentieth time I had been in a gym in my life. Not only did I have no clue what he wanted from me, but I thought at first that he wanted to borrow money. I walked over and stood over him, his face looking at mine, and said, "What would you like for me to do?"

"Well, Dr. Henry, I'm getting ready to lift this 410 pounds, and I'm going to press it a few times. Then I'm going to need your help in getting it back into the rack."

I thought it was appropriate at that time to inform him that standing in front of him was a 40-year-old, 145-pound man. If that weight happened to fall on him, the only way I could get it off would be to roll it down his body, which would be very uncomfortable, to say the least.

He laughed. "No, Dr. Henry, I don't need that much help. I just want you to help me steady the weight. As I'm lifting this weight, there will come a time when I can't do it, and I'll want you to help me put it in the rack."

I had read about women who, in times of panic, were able to lift automobiles off their children. But I've got to tell you, the connection between me and this student wasn't quite strong enough to expect that kind of response from me. Nevertheless, I agreed to help him. The funny thing was that during this process I found myself in the role of a cheerleader. Unracking the weight, he pressed it once, twice, then a third, fourth, and fifth time.

As he tried for the sixth time he got that "ugly" face. If you're not familiar with people who press weights, the ugly face is when the skin looks as though it's going to roll right off the skull. I could tell that this lift was a challenge.

What that young man did next scared me to death. He set the weight, the 410-pound weight, on his chest and started to breathe heavily—in, out, in, out. I had seen this before. I had been present at the birth of both of our children. That's when it occurred to me that perhaps I was on the wrong end of the operation.

But as he breathed a final time he made the ugly face, pushing the weight about four inches off his chest and arching his back slightly. In a calm voice he said, "OK." I steadied myself and tried to summon all my energy and focus on this weight. I wrapped my fingers around the bar, and he and I set the weight into the rack. I lifted maybe five pounds.

I'm a good teacher. And to be a good teacher, one must be a good student, be able to watch and learn. Once you learn, you must be able to apply what you've learned so that what you've just learned will be permanent.

I sat down next to this young man on the weight bench. As he wiped his face I said, "You know, I feel as though I've just learned a lesson, but I'm not really sure I know what that lesson is."

He looked at me, puzzled. "Dr. Henry, I'm not quite sure I understand."

"Well, let me review the process. I watched you lift that weight five times, and I, like you, was pretty confident you could do it. I was cheering you on. And then the sixth time came, and I could sense that it was tough. But even I knew that when you brought the weight to your chest it wasn't going to come up the seventh time. And I think you knew it too, but you tried it anyway."

He smiled and said, "The seventh one was the only one that did me any good. To build a muscle, you must exhaust it. And only when you exhaust that muscle will that muscle grow."

And that's when I understood the lesson: It's easy to deal with people in the morning, when we have lots of patience, lots of understanding, lots of energy. The problem comes later in the afternoon, you know, toward 5:00. That's when our patience runs thin, when we react instead of responding. Instead of showing our integrity level, we show our shortness of temper. What this young man was teaching me was that to be able to exercise these muscles, to be able to send down a root system that will bear a lot of weight, one must first exhaust the muscle so that it will grow.

A few weeks later I was driving from Greeneville, Tennessee, to Newport to teach class. I have always prided myself about being on time, but on this particular day I was running a little behind schedule. The curvy road running between Greeneville and Newport has a 55-mile-per-hour speed limit, but I almost defy you to try to drive it at that speed. You can go 55 mph, but I don't think you can do it with four wheels on the ground. Even so, I decided I would try to make up some time, and drove a little faster than usual. And I was doing a pretty good job. As a matter of fact, I thought I was going to make my class on time.

Then a man on a John Deere tractor appeared in front of me.

I know this man saw me. I'm pretty sure he heard me, because with each turn of the wheel my tires would squeal. He looked right at me. He looked left. He looked right. And then, when I was about 25 yards away, he pulled out.

I had to stand the car on its nose to stop in time. I was almost positive that even though this man had looked at me, he had not seen me. So I decided to blow my horn gently, just to let him know that I was back there. It turned out to be one of those longer-than-you-intended horn honks. It probably lasted about eight seconds. He stuck out his arm and motioned me around.

Now, in every free country on this planet such an arm motion means to come on around. And I thought that's what he wanted me to do. So I moved into the other lane and started to pass the tractor. Unfortunately, the only 18-wheeler I saw that day was coming toward me. I took that as some kind of indication that the man didn't want me to pass him. So I pulled in behind the tractor again and followed it down the road for 25 minutes at about 15 mph.

I was hot! No, that's not entirely correct—I was furious! When I got to the class, I told my students about this man and his John Deere tractor. I got home that night and spent 25 or 30 minutes explaining to my wife about this man on the John Deere tractor. When I went to work the next day, it was almost lunchtime before I had finished telling everybody about this man on the John Deere tractor.

And that's when it hit me. That's when I realized that the man on the John Deere tractor was literally occupying every free thought that I had. You might say that he was in control of my conscious thought. I wondered if I, somehow, was occupying his conscious thought. I don't think so. When we *react* to others instead of *responding* to them, we begin to manifest a behavior that is very contradictory to being responsive and very contradictory to a leadership style that shows integrity.

When I come to a strange town and walk to the front desk at the hotel, sometimes I can see by the clerk's face that the question I have just asked has been asked at least a thousand times before. You know the clues: the rolling of the eyes, the upward glance, the body language that says "This has to be the thousandth time I've been asked this question." The reason this happens is that the clerk doesn't realize that it's the first time *I* have asked that question. The clerk may have been asked that question a thousand times, but not by *me*.

It's the lifting of the weight. If it's the first time, it's fresh. But for some reason the last time makes it tough. Maybe the reason this happens is that we're stuck in *me*. Whether we want to admit this or not, we are our own favorite person. I guarantee you that we think more about ourselves than we do any other person on the planet.

Not long ago I was at the dedication of a brand-new hotel. A client had asked me to come and speak about service, which I'm always eager to do since it's one of my favorite topics. As I relaxed on a couch in the lobby of this beautiful Marriott property, watching people, a couple walked by. I heard them make a remark about the elevator. It went something like this: "You know, I believe that's the slowest elevator I've ever been on." The comment hit me as strange, but within the next 10 minutes two more people came by having the same conversation.

It started me thinking: *This is my client. I'm talking about service. If there's an issue with the elevator, maybe it's something I can talk about.* So I walked over to the front desk and asked the young clerk if they were having some problems with the elevator. I got the eye roll, followed by "Oh, if I have one more person ask me about the elevators and why they're so slow, I think I'll scream!"

"H'mmm," I said. "Have you had someone look at the elevators?"

"Oh, we've had people in here, but they can't seem to find anything wrong. And to be honest with you, sir, it's driving me nuts."

Being an old college professor, I thought I'd do a little research on my own. So I got on the elevator and rode up the 25 stories, timing it as the elevator climbed to the top. I got off and let the elevator go. Then I pushed the recall button and timed it. When it arrived, I got in and timed its descent to the lobby.

I went across the street to another hotel and got on their elevator.

Since this hotel was two stories taller, I went only to the twenty-fifth floor. I timed it, got out, and let the elevator go. Then I recalled it and rode the elevator down to the lobby. Interestingly enough, the elevator in this hotel was slower. It was puzzling. So I went to the front desk and asked the clerk, "Are you having any problems with the elevator?"

"No, we're not. But I understand the people at the Marriott are."

Bad news tends to travel quickly. I returned to the Marriott, unsatisfied with my experiment. I took another elevator ride and got a time very similar to the first one. Once again the elevator was faster than in the hotel across the street.

I rode the elevator up to the sixth floor and sat down on some very nice chairs in the elevator lobby and looked around. Something was missing! It almost leaped out at me. I went back downstairs and again walked up to the front desk. "May I speak to your general manager, please?"

The eye roll again. "You're not going to complain about the elevators again, are you?"

"No, ma'am, I'm not," I assured her. "As a matter of fact, I think I know what's wrong with your elevators."

"You wait right here, and I'll get him!"

In short order the general manager stepped out, putting his jacket on as he approached. "I understand you work for an elevator company."

I laughed. "No, sir, not at all, but I do think I know what's wrong with yours."

"If you can fix my elevator, you will make my day!" he exclaimed.

"Come with me," I invited.

We went up to the sixth-floor elevator lobby and sat down in two nice wing chairs.

"OK," he said. "Tell me what's wrong."

"Sir, you have nothing wrong with your elevator."

"What do you mean, we don't have anything wrong with our elevator?" he objected. "We get constant complaints about it!"

I held up my hand. "I don't think it's your elevator. Your problem, I believe, is in your elevator lobbies. There are no mirrors in your elevator lobbies."

"Mirrors? What does a mirror have to do with the speed of our elevators?"

I said, "Nothing at all. But mirrors are what we look into when we're waiting for the elevator. Because we're spending time with our best friend—which is, of course, ourselves—it occupies the time and makes that waiting time go by quicker."

He smiled in comprehension. "You know, we had mirrors in the elevator lobbies of the hotel property I was at before coming to this one."

"And I'll bet you had no complaints."

He laughed. "No, we didn't."

When we are responsive instead of reactive, everything seems to go smoother. It's not the mode we're in when we're responsive that gets us in trouble; it's the mode we're in when we're reactive that gets us in trouble. It causes us to do funny things and to make decisions in funny ways. It also affects our integrity, and we make wrong choices more often. If you're like me, you have probably wrestled with a decision. It's not so much the decision—we know what's right and what's wrong. Our brains almost automatically go there. The problem in the decision-making process is "Do I want to pay the price?"

The price of a right decision sometimes is tough. It's uncomfortable. But that doesn't make it any less right. The decision-making process isn't usually one of deciding what's right and what's wrong. It's a process of deciding which decision is the more comfortable.

I can remember kerosene lamps. I think we still have a few in our house. There is a control knob on the side of a kerosene lamp that controls the wick, and the length of the wick controls the height of the flame. As we work in our chosen profession, many times we take that control knob and turn it back just a hair. *No one will know this,* we think. *No one really pays attention to what I do. I do this little thing every day, and you know what? Today I'm just not going to do it.* And guess what? Nobody notices that we cut back a little bit. Oh, the flame height is barely noticeable. But as we do it again and again over a span of time, we've become a quitter. We're not involved anymore. We just go to work.

Let me take you through a little exercise. Let's pretend for a moment that you've been fired. Immediately there are two reactions to this phrase. The first reaction, of course, is that we're upset. After all, we depend on this income for a living. We depend on this job to support us and our families. So there's a bit of depression involved here. There's another reaction, and sometimes it's a good one: "Yes!" we say.

But I don't want to take you to that one. I want you to focus for a moment on thinking about losing your job. Now you're unemployed. So here is my proposal to you: Let's pretend that I want you to come work for me, doing exactly what you had been doing, making exactly the same amount of money. I have a question that I want you to answer: If you came to work for me—your new boss—tomorrow, would you work a little harder? Of course you would! You'd work a little harder because you have a new boss. You'd work a little harder because you want to make a good impression.

Now let's take out the firing part, and let me ask you another question: Couldn't you go into work tomorrow and work a little harder? Couldn't you go into work tomorrow and turn up the flame a bit? Couldn't you go to work tomorrow and, instead of turning the wick down, crank it up a bit? If we did that, we wouldn't hear this phrase so often: "Well, I'm all burned out." I don't like that phrase. When I hear that, I want to walk up to people and say, "You know what? I don't think you've ever been lit."

There are two variables hidden within this exercise. The first variable, of course, is that I just enabled you to respond to a situation. You took yourself through a conscious effort of thinking *What would it be like to lose my job? What would it be like to be fired?* That's not good. But if we fire ourselves every day, then we have to go in tomorrow and work a little harder, because, after all, we're working for a new boss.

The integrity side of this equation is that in reality that's what we're supposed to do. We're supposed to give those people who employ us an honest day's work. You may not like them, but that's not the issue. Your boss may not always be right, but he's the boss. Every single day we get to make a conscious effort to show those around us that we have integrity. Instead of reacting to situations, we respond to them.

In a way, our life is a lot like an airplane. If we were the pilot, we would make sure that the plane was maintained. We would make sure that every component in that plane worked properly. We would make sure that the weather we were flying in would be good weather. And we would make sure that the people who were helping us in the flying process were all performing to their utmost ability.

How would you feel if everybody who had anything to do with that flight looked at life in the way many of us look at life, and said, "See this little thing? I do this little thing every day. But today I'm not going to do it"? If enough people didn't do the little things they were supposed to do, the plane wouldn't be that safe. If the plane were going down, what would you do? Well, of course, it would be a little late then, wouldn't it?

Through using our responsiveness and integrity and turning our wick up a bit, we can learn to be like the bamboo tree. What we do every day affects those around us. We may never see growth in those people, but if we maintain our course, if we keep applying the right amount of cultivation and water, the people around us will be positively affected, and we'll see growth.

Like the young man in the weight room, we all must do our best and then stretch ourselves to go a little bit further. We can't allow people around us to control our thoughts. We are in control. Regardless of whether it's been a good day or a bad day, we need to *make* it a good day. We can't quit. We can't turn the wick back. And we need to make every decision for all the right reasons, not because they are easy to follow through.

In reality, we all fly the plane. We are all pilots, mechanics, co-pilots, and flight attendants. And by doing our job to the best of our ability, we make sure that those people who are riding along with us see us doing the right thing.

RECOGNIZE!

4

Recognize Your Understanding

Foolish leaders see through people.
Wise leaders see people through.

Trust in the Lord with all your heart and lean not on your own understanding.—PROVERBS **3:5.**

Adults sometimes play games. Unlike the games of our youth, these games aren't fun. They hurt others. We don't intend to hurt them. That, of course, is not our objective in playing these games; nevertheless, they do hurt those around us. What we will be discussing in this chapter is the importance of being humble in leadership.

I was doing a program in Jefferson City, Missouri. The following day I had to be in Kansas City, where I would be doing a program for the Social Security office. I went to the airport, presented my ticket to the ticket agent, and said, "Hey! How are you doing today? I'm going to Kansas City."

"Not on this plane, you're not," she said.

"What do you mean?"

"Well, it's snowing in St. Louis."

"That's not a problem for me," I assured her, "because I'm going to Kansas City."

"To get to Kansas City, you first must go through St. Louis," she said, which didn't make a whole lot of sense to me, but then sometimes air travel doesn't make sense. More often than not, air travel dictates that you must go east to fly west.

I said, "But, you see, it's important that I get to Kansas City, because I'm doing a program tomorrow."

"Well, sir, why don't you rent a car?" she suggested.

"How long a drive is it?" (When you travel around the country a lot, sometimes you forget your geography.)

"It's about a 90-minute drive from here."

Go figure: it was a two-hour flight but a 90-minute drive. Unfortunately, she had told 350 other folks the same thing she told me. Consequently, there were no cars to rent. There were no taxis or limos. And there were no U-Hauls. Yes, I called U-Haul. The woman said, "I just gave my last truck to two guys going to Kansas City."

There are times in your life when you rely on other individuals to help you. This was one of those occasions. At that time I had a young woman named Penny working in my office. Whenever I'm on the road and don't know what to do next, I rely on people to help me through those processes. So I called Penny.

"Penny, I'm trying to get to Kansas City for the program tomorrow. There are no planes, rental cars, taxis, or limos. And there are no U-Hauls. Penny, get me to Kansas City!"

"Sit down," she instructed.

As I've said, I've been married for more than 27 years. When a woman tells me to sit down, I sit down.

"I'm going to call you back in about five minutes. Stay right where you are."

Three minutes later the phone rang, and Penny said, "Here's what I want you to do. Walk about half a mile, turn right, and go three blocks. Turn left and go two blocks. Turn right, go one block, and you'll be there."

"Penny, where are you sending me?"

"Greyhound," she said.

I don't remember saying "Thank you" or "I appreciate it" or "Hey, you're great!" I do, however, remember what I was thinking:

I don't ride the bus. I'm not going to ride the bus. There is no way on God's green earth that I'm getting on the bus!

Before you think the wrong thing here, let me tell you that I was a sophomore in high school before we got indoor plumbing. I was not raised with a silver spoon in my mouth, and our family never had a lot of money. So why do I have a problem with riding the bus? Well, a couple of reasons. Number one, I once rode a bus from San Antonio, Texas, to Biloxi, Mississippi, crunched between two of the biggest, sweatiest guys I had ever seen. As I stepped off that bus I remember looking to the good Lord above and saying, "I hope You took a picture, because I'm not ever getting on another bus."

But that wasn't the reason I wasn't riding the bus. It wasn't the reason for my rudeness to Penny. I had had some success. I had some prosperity now. I was doing well. And in the words of my grandmother, I had gotten just a little bit too big for my britches. The reason I didn't want to ride the bus was that I thought I was too good to ride the bus. I thought, *I am not going to get on that bus. I'm not going to ride the bus. There is no way Dale Henry is going to ride a bus!*

I said this to myself all the way to the bus station. This game that I was playing—that we're so good at playing—was "poor, poor, pitiful me." Have you ever played this game? You know, when something happens around the office, when someone gives you an assignment that you feel is beneath you or that doesn't fit your image of what you think you do. We play this game—"poor, poor, pitiful me"—and I was playing it.

The problem with this game is that you can play it only for about 10 minutes. It becomes so stressful, so irritating to our souls, that after about 10 minutes the game changes from "poor, poor, pitiful me" to "If I ain't happy, ain't nobody going to be happy!" And I started plotting action in my head: *When I get to the bus station, when I walk into that Greyhound waiting room, I'm going to rip the head off the first person I meet and spit down their neck. I am going to be the customer everybody dreads to have. I'm not going to be pleasant, because I have to ride the bus!*

Arriving at the bus station, I pushed open the door, which caused a little bell to ring. If you have ever been in an establishment with a bell, you know how irritating that *tinkle, tinkle, tinkle* is. I thought, *The second I rip off the first person's head and spit down their neck, I'm going to shove this bell down the hole!*

That didn't happen. The second I pushed open the door, a voice called out, "Dr. Henry, it's good to have you at Greyhound!" *Dr. Henry? Penny must have briefed everybody!* A man walked over and took the luggage out of my hand. *Did you hear what I said? He took the luggage out of my hand!* (At the airport they won't even take your luggage until you answer a silly question: "Has anyone unknown to you handled your luggage?" If they were unknown to me, how would I know that they did anything?)

Taking my luggage, he said, "Dr. Henry, why didn't you call us from the airport? We would have sent a car to pick you up!"

All the while, I'm thinking, *If you had done that, I couldn't have played "poor, poor, pitiful me." I couldn't have had all that stress. I couldn't have had all that anxiety. I couldn't have had that vein on the side of my neck pop up to about the size of a rope big enough that you could have given me an IV from the opposite end of the bus station.*

The man said, "Dr. Henry, I know you're probably hungry after that walk. There's a really nice little café right down the block. Let me call and see what kind of special they have today." He got on the phone and talked for a moment. Then, covering the mouthpiece with his hand, he said, "Meat loaf. Do you like meat loaf?"

I said, "Oh, man! I *love* meat loaf! I'm from the South. Meat loaf is like manna from heaven for me! Tell them meat loaf, mashed potatoes, gravy on the side, green beans, a piece of apple pie, and a cold glass of milk."

"OK, Dr. Henry," he said, "you've got 45 minutes—plenty of time to go down and eat a snack. I know you have at least 45 minutes, because I called the bus driver."

Once again, let's review the airport scenario. You'll never walk up to a ticket agent at the airport and hear them say, "Your plane will be here in 45 minutes. I know, because I just called the pilot." The closest you will ever get to that statement is "The plane is in range." Does that mean that it's landing, or that they're going to shoot it down? I've been on some planes that were "in range" and, believe me, I've almost wanted them to shoot it down.

When I got to the café, a nice young woman had my lunch already on the counter. I sat down and had a wonderful meal as she and I talked. Thirty minutes later the phone rang. She picked it up and said, "Yes indeed, Walter, I'll tell him. Thanks." She turned to me and announced, "Your bus is here."

What are the chances, if I were sitting in Ruby Tuesday's at the airport, enjoying a sandwich, that the plane would take off and leave me there? I'd never hear over the loudspeaker, "Dr. Henry, your plane is here." When I returned, I saw my luggage being gently placed on the bus. You heard me right, I said gently. None of this watch-me-hit-that-little-hole-from-25-feet stuff, and the next thing you know, your drawers are rolling down the runway.

You're never going to guess where I sat on that bus. First class. Oh, you didn't know the bus had first class, huh? The front seat of the bus is better than first class on a plane. On the front seat of the bus you can see the bus driver. If you're sitting in first class on a plane, you can't see the pilot. They shut that little door. Did you ever give any thought to that? Did you ever wonder why they shut that little door? Well, I'll tell you why. Because there's not anybody up there! You see, during those few minutes right before the plane backs up, the pilots crawl out that little window. And have you ever wondered why it takes them so long to get that jetway up against the plane? It's to give them time to get two more pilots back in the plane through that little window. Pay attention, because it's never the same two guys.

But there I was, in first class on the front seat on the bus. The nice woman behind me was going from St. Louis to Kansas City to visit her schoolteacher daughter. She tapped me on the shoulder. "You don't ride the bus much, do you?"

I said, "Ma'am, why would you ask me a question like that?"

"People just don't wear suits on the bus anymore. But I think you look nice. Are you hungry?"

"You know, ma'am, I could always eat a little something," I said.

"How about a peanut butter cracker?"

"Yeah, I like peanut butter crackers." I thought she was going to hand me a little pack of peanut butter crackers, but that didn't happen at all. She took out a big foursquare cracker and a jar of peanut butter and a knife, and made it right there on the spot! She squished the two sides of that peanut butter cracker together (I was really glad she didn't lick the edges) and handed it to me. I started to take a bite. I'm from the South. I love hospitality.

She held up her hand. "Oh, honey, please don't eat that yet! That will make you half gag. You've got to have something to drink with it."

I stopped midbite. "Well, what have you got?"

"What do you want?"

"How about a root beer?"

"I've got a root beer right here." She reached in a cooler, pulled one out, and handed it to me.

Please take this picture. I'm in first class on a bus, riding to Kansas City. I've got a complimentary peanut butter cracker and a complimentary root beer. On a plane you don't get even peanuts anymore. (Oh, somebody's allergic.) What you get is something they call a mix, or pretzels. Either way, it's not edible. I've had pretzels. What you get on a plane are not pretzels. I've had a mix. What you get on a plane definitely isn't a mix. After you eat a pack, it hangs in your throat like a big lump. After a while a flight attendant will come by and say, "Would you like a little refreshment?" This is the only place on the planet where you can serve 63 people out of a single can of soda. You are forced to stick your tongue down in the small hole of the ice to get any moisture at all.

I looked over at the bus driver, whose name was Willy according to his name tag, and said, "Hey, Willy! How long have you been driving a bus?"

He said, "Which time? I drove a bus for 15 years and had to stop."

"How come?" I asked.

"I went blind."

That's an important thing to know about your bus driver—can he see? I said, "You're kidding me, right, Willy?"

"No, I'm not at all. I drove a bus for 15 years, came in one day to work, and my vision was a little blurry. I went to the eye doctor and found out I had a strange cornea disease. In six months, almost to the day, I was blind."

"Wow, Willy! That must have been weird!" An uneasy feeling was rising in my throat.

"You know the first thing I did, sir?"

"No. What, Willy?"

"I started to play a game—'poor, poor, pitiful me.' I had planned to go to my high school reunion, but I was so embarrassed about not being able to see that I didn't go. A young woman, who now lives in Atlanta, came to the high school reunion and also to our church. She recognized me and slid over next to me in the pew. We started to talk, and as the good Lord sometimes does, He put that young woman in my church to help me.

"She worked for an eye specialist in Atlanta, Georgia. They had been experimenting with some new procedures, and she gave me her card. I called, Dr. Henry, and I drive a bus today because two people who were eye donors died. I have the eyes of two people in my head."

I said, "That's an incredible story."

He handed me his wallet, which looked like a small portfolio. In it I saw a picture of an attractive young woman and a handsome young man. "Are these your children, Willy?"

"No," he said quietly. "Those are the people whose eyes made it possible for me to see."

"That had to be a very painful surgery. I know my wife had her eye scratched once while roller skating. I remember the intense pain she went through. She cried almost all night long. And I know the eye is one of those things you can't do a lot with as far as pain relief."

"Yes," he admitted, "it was uncomfortable."

Uncomfortable? I thought. *More like very painful.* "Are there any side effects, anything that has been very difficult for you?"

"Well, there is one thing, but it's hardly worth mentioning. Every time I go to the beach my right eye looks at all the girls, and my left eye—"

Before he finished, the woman behind me patted me on the back and laughed. "He got you on that one, didn't he?"

What an amazing man! I tell you this story to let you again take a picture. I want you to see the front of the bus. On the left-hand side is a man who always wanted to be a bus driver, like his father. He said he loved the people and liked to travel and serve others.

On the right-hand side of the bus, on the front seat, was a man who thought he was too good to ride on the bus. That's pretty sad, isn't it? But that's what games make us do. Games we play as adults tend to test the true mettle of our leadership. We cannot be the prize if, during times of success, we lose our focus on leading by focusing on our own needs, by allowing ourselves to get too big for our britches. We have to affirm to ourselves goals that strengthen our capacity to give to others. And through that strengthening we will become the prize, and we will have knowledge and be able to lead.

One of the funniest things about that bus trip to Kansas City was that the taxi I took from the bus station to my hotel cost more than the bus ride from Jefferson City to Kansas City.

If you have checked into a hotel very late at night, you're accustomed to being treated, I won't say rudely, but—well, the clerk may be a little short with you. Let me tell you why that happens. The person who is taking care of you and giving you service is not a desk clerk. If you arrive late at night, the person who gives you service is a night auditor, an accountant, a person who is hired by the hotel to do the books late at night. How would you feel if your primary job was to be an accountant, and every 10 minutes somebody disturbed you to be checked into a hotel? You probably wouldn't be the most friendly person in the world.

As I walked into the Courtyard by Marriott and swung open the door, I heard this: "Dr. Henry! Welcome to the Courtyard by Marriott! Hey, how was your bus ride?"

I was baffled. "How did you know my name?"

"Penny called. She said you'd be arriving a little late."

I was tired. It had been a busy day. But this young woman had such a gift, one that almost every woman knows about. (The second that women hear this two-word phrase, "company's coming," they get a little knot in their stomach. They will go to their home and want to clean it. And when that guest comes to the door, they'll say, "If I had known you were coming, I would have cleaned up!")

This young woman's name was Lena, and Lena knew how to take care of company when company was coming. She said, "I know a little bit about you." She knew my name, what I did for a living, why I was in Kansas City, about the program I was doing, the client I was doing it for, and the conference room in which I was going to be speaking. She knew my wife's name and that my wife was a teacher. She knew each of my children's names and knew their hobbies. Lena knew all this information about someone who was going to be staying at her hotel for two days.

That's what "company's coming" does to you. That's what being a leader does for you. And that's what knowledge will do for you. It sets the stage for service. It makes you the guide.

As I started to turn away, Lena said, "Dr. Henry, I almost forgot! You're a runner. You like to run, right?"

"Why, yeah, I love to run."

"What time would you like to wake up in the morning?"

I left a wake-up call, and she smiled again. She took out two free breakfast coupons, signed her name to the bottom, and said, "While you're here at my hotel, Dr. Henry, you'll be eating on the house."

Do you think I went to bed tired? Do you think I went to bed upset over the day's travel? No, I didn't! I went to bed refreshed, feeling blessed that I had met a leader and a prize. The next morning I went out and ran. Then I decided to eat breakfast. With my free coupon in my pocket, I went into the restaurant.

I don't like to eat by myself, and I spotted a man who was getting ready to eat.

"Sir, would you mind if I join you? I hate to eat by myself. Food just does not digest properly when you're eating by yourself. Another smiling face makes that food go down so much easier."

"Of course! Please join me," he invited.

I sat down and ordered my meal.

He said, "You know, I know a little about you."

"Did Penny call you, too?" I asked.

"No. But I do know that you got here last night somewhere between 11:30 and 12:30."

"You're right!"

"I know that when you came into the hotel you met a young woman whose name is Lena."

"You're right again!"

"I also know that the breakfast you're getting ready to eat is on the house."

"You're good!" I said with admiration.

"No, I just know Lena. I work for a little greeting card company near here, and I come to Kansas City about three days a week. I could stay anywhere I want, but I choose to stay here. Oh, it's a nice hotel, but that's not why. I stay here because of Lena. You might not know this, but Lena doesn't work the night shift."

"Yes, she does. I saw her last night."

"No," he said. "Lena comes in for an hour every night so that her auditor can have an hour to eat."

I said, "When I get through eating my breakfast, I'm going to go tell the manager what a gift he has here. What a wonderful employee he has in Lena!"

"She would like that."

I stopped at the front desk after breakfast and asked to speak to the general manager. I said, "Sir, I know this is a very busy time of the day for you, and I won't take up a lot of your time, but I want to compliment you on one of your employees."

His upraised hand stopped further words. "Lena, right? It's always Lena. Lena, Lena, Lena. Let me tell you about Lena. She came to work for me about 15 years ago. Twenty times she came, putting in an application and asking for a job. As a matter of fact, she came in 20 days straight. And for 20 days straight I said no. We have a policy here that we don't hire folks without a high school diploma. But Lena wouldn't give up. So I gave her a job in housekeeping. I thought there she would be of little harm to anyone, and no one would ever know.

"But I didn't know Lena. Before long Lena had gotten her GED. She had gone from working in housekeeping to being the head of housekeeping. But that wasn't enough for Lena. She went back and got her associate degree in hotel/motel management. Then she went from the head of housekeeping to the head of the restaurant. Even that wasn't enough for Lena. She went back and got her Bachelor's degree in hotel/motel management, and before I knew it, she was head of food and beverage. Then she was the head of the sales department. And, sir, she is now my assistant general manager. Lena is after my job."

I said, "I hate to tell you this, but I think she's going to get it."

He shook his head. "Well, either you're very wise or a good guesser."

I said, "I don't understand."

"I'm going to be the general manager of the new property we have in St. Louis. I didn't know until the fax came in this morning who would be taking my job. The new general manager at this property will be Lena."

Lena was a prize. Willy, the bus driver, was a prize. If you want to be the prize, you have to check your vision. If you're spending your time seeing through people, you're going to play games. You're going to be upset. Your day is not going to go well, and you're going to be miserable. But if you spend your day seeing people through, you'll be a prize and will be counted as a blessing.

5

Recognize Your Control

Pygmalion partnerships: Living up to the expectations we place on others!

A kind man benefits himself, but a cruel man brings trouble on himself.—PROVERBS **11:17**.

Loving someone doesn't give us the right to try to mold them into someone we want them to be. Love is one of those things we often misunderstand. The first lie about marriage is that it is 50-50. Marriage is 100-0. It's 100 percent loving, 100 percent giving, 100 percent understanding, while expecting nothing in return.

I don't think I really understood this until we had our first baby, when my wife laid our small pink daughter in my arms. I never thought I would fall in love with a toothless, bald-headed woman, but here lay this innocent, helpless creature in my arms. That small baby could do nothing for me, but I loved her with the purest kind of love I had ever experienced. Four years later Debra laid another baby girl in my arms, and I understood then that love is not doled out in measure—it's all-inclusive; it's giving 100 percent all the time. Expect nothing; give everything.

Love and time have an interesting connection. For some, love fades over time; for others, it seems only to grow. Several years ago I was asked to speak at a large church in Arkansas. Later we had dinner at the church, and I met some of the members one-on-one.

When an elderly man joined our little group at our table, one of my new friends asked him how he had enjoyed my presentation. He smiled politely and looked at me. "Well, to tell you the truth," he said, "I don't remember everything you said. But I remember that I liked it."

A young woman in the group chimed in, "Oh, I remember *everything*—all the stories, all the laughter . . . I loved it!"

The old man looked at her. "Could you do me a favor? Would you take this wicker basket and fill it with water for me?"

The woman seemed a little confused. "Wicker doesn't hold water."

Without looking up, the old man said, "No, but the basket becomes a little cleaner every time you do it."

Time diminishes many things, but the message of love cleans all of us. In times of change and stress, real prizes give those around them the one true gift of love.

Time. It is what we most need to share, because our time is what the people we love need most.

Since I believe that every chapter in this book should be loaded with useful advice to help people improve their relationships, I can offer, from my wealth of experience, useful information about getting your kids ready for church. If you have children, you know that by the time everybody is ready for church you have lost all the religion that you had. You've probably broken three or four of the Ten Commandments and are closing in on "Thou shalt not kill."

It's important to me that I get to church on time. So the night before, I go into my kids' rooms and pick out what I want them to wear. The next morning I throw their clothes and them, naked, into the minivan. They always get ready then, because in the South people simply don't go to church naked. This tactic works on every single soul in my family except Debra, my wife—the ringleader.

I love my wife more than anything else, but Debra does not like to be on time. It's not her thing. She really believes that she can take a bath 15 minutes before we're to be somewhere and actually get dressed and make it on time. We had tried pretty much everything to get her to be on time.

For a moment I'd like to talk specifically to the male readers. Men, there are many things we can do to try to speed up our wives' processes of getting ready. One of those, though, is not blowing the horn. Blowing the horn won't get them ready any quicker. What it will do is make you miss out on the only good home-cooked meal you will get that day.

I remember the good old days when Mother used to step out on the back porch and say, "It's time to eat!" All of us would run to the table and sit down and eat. My wife steps out on the back porch and says, "It's time to eat!" and we all get in the minivan and go to dinner. I remember saying at a meal, "This is just like Mama used to make." My girls no doubt will say, "This is just like Cracker Barrel used to make."

Like I said, we had tried pretty much everything to get my wife ready for church on time, and nothing had worked. Not until one morning as my girls were getting dressed in the back of the van. My older daughter said, "Dad, we should try positive expectancy." She had heard a pastor preach a sermon on positive expectancy, and no doubt she was trying to apply some of that wisdom to my life.

"So what do you suggest we do?" I asked.

"Dad, we simply ought to expect Mom to be ready on time."

"OK," I said. "We've tried everything else; I don't know why we shouldn't try that."

So we composed a little song:

"Mama's going to be ready on time. Uh-huh!
Mama's going to get ready on time. Yeah!
Mama's going to be ready on time. Uh-huh!
Mama's going to get ready on time. Yeah!"

We sat in the van in the driveway and sang a few verses. *If nothing else,* I thought, *it would occupy some time until my wife came out.* But the second we started singing that song, my wife emerged from the garage, panty hose in one hand, shoes in the other. Until you've seen a full-grown woman put on a pair of panty hose in the front of a minivan, you have not lived. The first thing Debra did was throw her dress over her head.

"What are you doing?"

"I don't want people to know who I am."

Think about that for a minute. What are the chances somebody would pick up a hitchhiker with her dress over her head? And how could she explain our kids in the back seat? I ask you, who else is it going to be? The next step with the panty hose was the pull-tug-wiggle maneuver as she inserted her body. (Truly, panty hose are made of a miracle fabric. How anything can come out of a container the size of an egg and fit a human being's body is a genuine miracle!)

Then the dress came down, and we started off to church. As I was driving, paying attention to getting there and trying my best to hurry so we would be on time, my wife yelled in a loud, excited voice, "Stop the car! Stop the car!"

My first thought was that one of my children had fallen out of the car, and I came to a screeching halt.

"Didn't you see it?" she cried.

"Didn't I see what?"

She waved her hand toward the front of the car. "There's a turtle in the road."

"It's a turtle," I said.

"I don't want to see the poor thing get killed. Honey, won't you get out and move it off the road?"

I'm a country boy. I have spent my life having fun in the hills of Tennessee, and I've seen a lot of turtles. I could tell that this was a snapping turtle. Snapping turtles aren't friendly on any occasion. They're nasty little things. So that morning I decided that I would teach my wife a lesson. "Honey," I said, "why don't *you* get out of the car and move the turtle?"

My wife's not from the country. She's from California. I've been to California many times and don't recall ever seeing a snapping turtle there, so I was pretty sure Debra had never seen one either. So she got out of the car and, being a first-grade teacher, started talking to it. She bent down and cooed, "You're going to get run over out here."

I told the girls that it might be a good idea if they moved to the front of the car, because what was going to happen next was going to be quite entertaining.

As Debra reached down to take hold of the turtle's shell, the turtle looked up and jumped about two inches off the ground, trying to get to my wife before my wife got to it. During that two-inch jump my wife managed to get back in the car before the turtle's feet touched the pavement again. By now Debra was crying. "All I wanted to do was save the poor thing's life!"

I have a soft heart, and I love my wife, even though she can sometimes do things that drive me crazy. I said, "Honey, I will give you a lesson on snapping turtles." I got out of the car, picked up a stick from the side of the road, and poked it at the turtle. The turtle snapped and grabbed hold of the stick. I then pulled the turtle out of the road. I got back in the car, and we went to church—late, of course. (That's the only way we know how to get to church. The pastor doesn't even start until we get there. He knows that's his cue.)

We sit in the balcony. We began sitting in the balcony when our kids were small and noisy, and it's now become a ritual. I don't know your rituals at your place of worship, but let's see if they are anything like ours. In our church we stand up and sing; then we sit down. We stand up and sing; then we sit down. We stand up and pray; then we sit down. The pastor preaches, we stand up, and then we go home. That's pretty much our ritual.

This day we all stood up, and I was enjoying listening to my wife and daughters sing. They have beautiful voices that all blend together. Each voice is different, but somehow they make each other complete. (I'm not a very good singer, so I lip-synch.) At the end of the song we sat down. Counting our three years of courtship, I've been going to church with my wife a little more than 30 years. I have seen about every behavior from her that there is to be seen. At least I had until that morning.

After that first segment of singing and sitting down, my wife did something I had never seen her do before. As she sat down she scooted up, she scooted back, she scooted to the left, and she scooted to the right. I thought at first that a fabric softener sheet from the dryer had gotten someplace it shouldn't be. Being pretty smart, I decided to let it go and give her some time. After all, time is what most of us need when our loved ones do things we don't understand. If we don't take that time, most of us will end up saying things that will definitely not make us the prize in our marriage.

We got to the second stand-up-and-sing-then-sit-down part of church. I had forgotten all about my wife's little maneuver. I was reminded as she once again scooted up, scooted back, scooted to the left, and scooted to the right. You might have characterized it as the sitting version of the macarena.

The third portion of church is my favorite part. It's not because my pastor is so good at praying that you can sometimes catch a little nap. It's because of what my wife does: she hugs me as we pray. I can tell you right now that my heart goes pitter-patter when my wife embraces me, when she holds me and touches me. She completes me.

As she held me close that day I realized that sometimes when you get a little tickled at church, things become tremendously funny. We probably ought to laugh more often in church, but nobody laughed that day. As my wife held me close she was in a talkative mood. She whispered, "I think I know what's wrong with my panty hose."

The majority of men don't wear panty hose, and we really don't know much about them, even after years of seeing them hanging in the bathroom. I leaned into my wife and said, "Honey, what seems to be the problem with your panty hose?"

In kind of a giggly tone she said, "Well, this morning I was in a hurry to get ready, and I accidentally grabbed a pair of Lauren's panty hose." (Lauren at that time was 8 years old.)

That was the first I knew that panty hose came in different sizes. I said, "Honey, how do you know that you have on Lauren's panty hose?"

Indicating a location slightly above her knee, she said, "Because the top of my panty hose are right about there."

This struck me as tremendously funny. Not because my wife's panty hose were down around her knees. I thought it was funny because I know my wife's ritual. After the sermon my wife goes down to the lower part of our church and shakes people's hands. She works the crowd like a politician before Election Day. I usually take the kids, and we go out and get the car. But not that day. *Today, I was thinking, I think I'll walk around with Deb. Yep. This should be a Kodak moment. Because I know those puppies are coming down, and I want to be there.*

I followed my wife around all morning as she did her ritual, as she walked from place to place meeting and greeting folks. She didn't once let those panty hose come down. She didn't act any different than she would have if she had on the best-fitting pair of panty hose ever made.

When we got to the car she said, "I noticed you walked with me at church today."

"That's right," I said.

"I know that's not what you normally do, and I know why you did it," she said.

"What do you mean?" I asked innocently.

"You walked with me at church today because you thought my panty hose would come down."

Of course, I wasn't about to admit to anything. So I said, "Well, honey, I love you very much, and I know that underneath your cool and calm facade is a deep current flowing. You had reason this morning not to be cool and calm. But what I observed wasn't at all what I expected. As you walked around the church, greeting people, never once did you give any indication that there was anything wrong. You're my prize, honey. You're the person I was made to be with."

What she said next completely baffled me. She said, "Oh, I pulled up my panty hose several times during today's walk around the church."

"No, you didn't, honey, because I walked behind you. I stayed right with you, and I never saw you pull up anything."

"That's because you know absolutely nothing about panty hose. If you raise your knees, you can pull up your panty hose. If you have great thigh control, you can pull those panty hose up."

I know nothing about the advice my wife gave me that morning, because I have never worn a pair of panty hose. But I can tell you this: My wife is quite a woman. The good Lord must have loved me a lot, and I am pretty sure that it's the 100-0 kind of love. Oh, I'm sure He hopes we'll love Him back. But even if we don't, He loves us anyway.

We can create great responses in our loved ones by treating them as valuable, competent, and talented individuals. If we give time to the people we love, they will tell us what's wrong. But until we are able to give that time commitment, until we are able to love them unconditionally, we are never going to be blessed. We're never going to be recognized. We're never going to recognize that marriage and faith are all about love, the pure gift of being the prize.

▬ ▬ ▬ ▬ ▬ ▬ ▬ ▬ ▬ ▬ ▬ ▬ ▬ ▬ ▬ ▬ ▬ ▬ ▬ ▬

6

Recognize Your Family Involvement

Private living: Learning from the Master's teachers—our kids.

A wise son heeds his father's instruction, but a mocker does not listen to rebuke.—PROVERBS **13:1.**

Have you ever eaten at McDonald's? Silly question! Is there anyone who hasn't? Can you tell me why *adults* eat at McDonald's? Be careful—the real answer is not "Well, because my kids go there."

I've done an assessment. Let me take you through it. Adults eat at McDonald's because it's quick, easy, inexpensive, and convenient. And it's predictable. It's pretty much always going to be the same— no better, no worse.

Just for a moment, step out of your shoes. Why does a 5-year-old child eat at McDonald's? Oh, the reasons are quite different. First of all, here is a major organization, a Fortune 500 company—a huge conglomerate—whose major spokesperson is a clown.

OK, so you're thinking that you have that same problem where you work. In your case, somebody was hired who turned out to be a clown. McDonald's did it on purpose; they specifically hired a clown.

Second, a 5-year-old child doesn't eat at McDonald's because they serve a nutritious meal or because the food is great. No. It's because McDonald's has the Happy Meal. It's not about food. It's about happy. It's about an experience. McDonald's sells an experience. They sell fun. We could call it the Walt Disney World of food chains. Not only that, the Happy Meal comes with a prize, a toy. Another thing, take a look outside a McDonald's, and you'll usually see a playground.

Let's recap. Who is McDonald's' major customer? Kids are! Adults eat there too because it's quick, easy, convenient, inexpensive, and predictable.

Let's set up a simulation. Let's look at this ordinary event of eating at McDonald's in an extraordinary way and see if we can learn some answers to future questions. Here we go!

You are going to eat at McDonald's with a 5-year-old child, and you are in a hurry.

Now, what part of that sentence do you think a 5-year-old child would not understand? Correct! Hurry. I've never met a 5-year-old child who was in a hurry, because 5-year-old children do not understand the concept of time. They see time the way a dog sees time. When somebody rings the doorbell, a dog will immediately run to the door. Why? Is it for them? No, it's never for them, but they always run to the door and bark as if to say, "Hey! I'll get it! It's for me!"

Here's a little exercise. When you go home after work, watch your dog's behavior. He'll bark, he'll wag his tail, he'll run around. He's excited, as if to say, "Look, look! You're home! You're home!" Don't talk to the dog or say anything to him. Just shut the door and count to eight. Then open the door. What does the dog do? He runs around yapping, "Look! You're home! You're home!" Your dog doesn't know the difference between eight hours and eight seconds.

That's the way a 5-year-old child sees time. The child understands the concept, she just doesn't understand the measurement. So you're going to McDonald's with a 5-year-old child, and you're in a hurry. If you're a man, you say, "Let's go in real quick." (Men see life in a very simplistic way. We need this, we get it done, and we move on.) What part of "Let's go in real quick" does the 5-year-old not understand? To a child that sentence sounded like this: "We're going to go in, blah, blah, blah, blah." "Real quick" was not an understandable part of the sentence.

You run around the car and open the door, reach inside, and grab the child. You don't look at the child; you don't think about the child. You're thinking about being in a hurry. You never once turn around and look at the child, but lead her toward the goal of getting in and getting out.

The funny part of this little simulation is watching the child. Instead of running toward the goal, the child is looking left, right, behind, ahead. What is she looking for? The clown! She knows that clown is here somewhere. She's seen the commercial.

Once inside, you walk up to the counter, look at the child, and say, "What do you want?"

Mouth open, eyes wide, the child looks at the menu, then turns to you and says, "I can't read."

"Oh, I forgot! You want a Happy Meal, right? A Happy Meal with cheese. And a milk. OK, we've got it." You turn to the person behind the counter and say, "We want a Happy Meal. With cheese and a milk. I'll take anything. Upsize it; we're in a hurry."

It's easy, it's quick, it's convenient, it's inexpensive, and it's predictable. You hand the Happy Meal to the child and, running in front of her, say, "Let's go! We're in a hurry." Then you realize you're alone. Turning around, you see the child sitting on the floor, french fries all around her, hamburger lying to the side, and the toy package in her mouth. She's trying to tear the plastic wrapper away from the magic gem inside.

You run back. "No, no! Pick that up! We're in a hurry! We have to leave now!"

The small child will get to her feet, point outside, and say, "I want to go to the playground."

"We'll come back later," you say.

She's heard that line before. "No, I want to play now. Just for five minutes." Where did she get this "five minutes" thing? Where did she develop this bit of wisdom about time? She got it from you!

This small child, who has no concept or understanding of time, is using time to convince you to let her play.

"OK," you bargain. "Five minutes. But that's it. Then we have to leave, because we're in a hurry."

Do you believe in your heart that she's going to want to leave in five minutes? Of course not, because she doesn't understand time. She's going to negotiate for another five minutes, and then another five minutes. You stand out there negotiating with a 5-year-old child. "OK, one more time down the slide, and that's it. Don't ask again, because this is the last time down the slide."

Finally you look at her and say possibly the most stupid sentence any man has ever said in his entire life: "OK, I'm just going to leave you here."

Did it ever occur to you that that's exactly where she wants to be? Think about it. She has a Happy Meal. She knows that sooner or later that clown's going to show up. And in that Happy Meal is a prize around which McDonald's has put the food, as packing material, to keep the toy from being broken. The child will not eat the food. Children aren't there because of the food. They're there because of the prize. Even a child understands the prize. The prize is the best in us.

We are reminded that changing on the inside sustains momentum and can overpower setbacks. Looking at the little successes along the way with our family can help us keep on God's track.

How many of you can remember 1991? If you are having trouble, let me help you—Desert Storm. Ah, now that you have a focal point, you can remember. In 1991 my wife and I both were in the Air National Guard. In January of that year I was asked if I liked the beach. I didn't understand. They said, "Dale, lots of sand, not much water."

Because I was in a unit that was highly mobile, they asked us all to go home and make sure our affairs were in order. Bad news never comes at good times. We had been in the Guard for several years and knew there was a possibility that this could happen at any time, so we got ready.

The first weekend in February the phone was ringing when we came home from church. On the line was Chief Master Sergeant Soboleski, our first sergeant. In a very low voice the chief said, "Dale, how are you doing?"

"Fine, Sobi, but I can tell from the tone of your voice that this isn't a social call."

"You're right, Dale."

I said, "Sobi, if it's any consolation, we've been expecting the call."

"No," he said, "I don't think so. You see, Dale, Debra has just been activated."

Now, folks, when daddy gets called to war, that's one thing. But when mama gets called to war, she leaves you at home with the kids.

Because Debra was one of the first women activated in Desert Storm, she became an immediate hero. She was interviewed by all the local papers and the radio and was on all the local television channels. Everybody in our small community knew my wife. But what they did next almost scared me. People would come up to my wife, hold her by the arm or give her a hug, and say, "We're praying for you." Not one person ever said they would pray for me! Debra was going away, but I had to stay. I was probably the only one who had any chance of being killed in this whole exercise, because if anything happened to those kids, my wife would have killed me!

When my wife left, I cried. For lots of reasons. I cried because I would miss my wife, whom I love very much. Probably the biggest reason I cried, though, was that I was thinking about all the things I was going to have to do—dress the kids, feed the kids, take care of the house, do all the shopping . . . I was thinking about me—not Debra. I was trapped inside me.

I immediately started wondering how I could be a good mommy. I'd had a good mother. And my wife was a good mother, so I had two role models to be guided by. I thought, *The people in my community are going to see my children and me in church together. If they are going to see us in church together, what are they going to look for? How we are dressed.* (People notice our outside long before they notice our inside.)

I decided that my kids were going to look good. I got up at 6:00 a.m. and put my plan into effect. Early, sure, but have you ever tried to put panty hose on two little girls with their legs kicking around? I figured that while they were asleep and were good and still I could slip those babies on, and we'd be ready to go.

As I dug around in their closets I found two dresses wrapped in plastic. Why don't you women tell men little things such as "You're not supposed to wear white shoes until Easter"? I put those little Easter dresses on the girls, and I want you to know they looked great! They were so poofy and pretty. The only problem was that this was the second weekend in February. We walked into church, and I stood there holding the girls' hands and said, "You look good, girls! You look good."

Before long I knew I had messed up. My first clue was when the older women turned around, looked at me, and in a low voice said, "Bless his heart!" If you aren't familiar with this Southern term, it's basically the same as saying, "That looks pretty stupid, doesn't it?"

We walked down to the front row of the church and assumed our positions on the second pew. LeAnne, my older daughter, has always been a huggy child. She loves to hold on to her daddy. I've got to tell you, that makes my heart sing with joy. My younger daughter, Lauren, is an independent child. She is that child for whom the leash was invented. She's an independent thinker and an independent knower. Whenever she wants to do something, she is the first one there.

Lauren loved the children's sermon because she could run down to the front of the church, slide across the floor, and be the first one there. She's very competitive. When the pastor said, "Now all the children can come down to the front of the church," Lauren was usually the first one there.

But not on this morning. She knew she looked special. Instead of running, she stood up, grabbed the bottom of that dress, and started sashaying to the left and sashaying to the right. She did a couple of turns, and then the pastor saw her. He knew that her mother had just been activated, and he wanted to make her feel special. So he looked at my child and said, "Lauren, you are so pretty! That is the most beautiful dress I have ever seen in my entire life."

Then my almost-3-year-old child, the gleam in her daddy's eye, walked right over to the pastor, grabbed the bottom of her dress and pulled it up almost over her head, and declared, "But my daddy likes the panties the best!"

You can't get that low in a church pew. But that's not what embarrassed me. What really embarrassed me was the fact that I didn't know that the frilly part of the panty hose went in the back. And that's when all the ladies in my church said in unison, "Bless his heart!"

They probably also thought, *I'll bet his house is a mess.* That's not fair. I'll have you know that you could eat off of our floors. There were mashed potatoes on one side and green beans on the other. That's when a dog comes in handy. Sandy could clean up the floor. I could set the baby on the floor, and Sandy would clean her face up. Sandy would even cheerfully clean our dishes up before we put them in the dishwasher. But you know what my kids did? They told on me when their mother came back. All the things we had done that I thought were in confidence.

I learned a lot in those six months that my wife wasn't there. Most of that learning took place because of my children. They made me a better father, and they made me a pretty decent mother. It took me a while to understand the real difference between a mother and a father. I think it's in the discipline area. We fathers want a quick, get-it-over-with kind of answer. But mothers try to teach a lesson.

One morning I got up early. My girls, on occasion, would wake up in a very bad mood. I don't know why that was, but this particular morning I was making French toast. If I may say so, I make the best French toast on the planet.

LeAnne came in and said loudly, "I want the first piece of French toast, and I want it now!"

Of course, that woke up the baby, and she said, "No! You got the first piece of French toast yesterday! I get the first piece of French toast today!" Then she looked at me. "Daddy! She touched my sleeve."

You all know how that goes. I wanted to teach them a lesson, and I thought, *I'll teach them like Debra would teach them.* I looked at my oldest child and said, "LeAnne, what would Jesus do?"

Putting her head down, she said, "Daddy, Jesus would let somebody else have the first piece of French toast."

I was very pleased. I was becoming a mommy, and a pretty good mommy at that. When I turned around to flip over the French toast, I saw my daughter bend down to her baby sister and say, "You get to be Jesus tomorrow."

We all want the good qualities of the Master—we just want someone else to exhibit them. I learn from my children. I always have. They teach me the values of being the prize. They teach me to recognize these values through family involvement, not just living with the family. Don't simply take your children places; interact with them when you go.

Sharing time in this hectic world is very important, especially with our children. I try my best to spend time with them individually so that I can get to know them, get to know their ways of thinking, and learn from them. They are my teachers. They are the Master's teachers. And you have no idea how proud I am to tell you that they are my kids!

INDIVIDUALIZE!

▬ ▬ ▬ ▬ ▬ ▬ ▬ ▬ ▬ ▬ ▬ ▬ ▬ ▬ ▬ ▬

7

Individualize Your Self-talk

Speaking your mind: Dealing effectively with those around you.

In his heart a man plans his course, but the Lord determines his steps.—PROVERBS 16:9.

When it comes to our minds and our self-talk, most of us think we have a pretty good handle on the way it works. Oh, you've heard it before: "If thoughts could kill . . ." Our thoughts do kill—they kill us. They kill us with stress and with unnecessary worry. But thoughts can also heal. Positive thoughts can make you feel better.

Or how about this one: "If they could read my mind . . ."

Here's one of my favorites: "Boy, I'd love to give him a piece of my mind." (In some cases, we've already given too much of it away.)

Our minds have four motives, four ways of looking at situations. These four motives of our minds are like swords. We can use them not only to hurt others but also to help them, by cutting through all the webs that the mind imposes on us, those entanglements that, if left unchecked, can control us.

Our minds, if properly controlled, can be tremendously effective. Our minds can be caring, and unfortunately, they also can be very conniving and extremely careless. As we discuss these four motives of our minds, try to put yourself into the situations. Try to see how easily we obey our minds.

You're going to say, "Uh, Dale, that's not the way it works. I control my mind." Well, I would hope that's true, but most of the time it's not—it's the complete opposite. Have you ever gotten up in the morning and said, "You know, I really don't feel very well," and gone through the day carrying out that simple thought? You don't feel well, so you walk and talk as though you don't feel well. Your posture shows others that you don't feel well, and they ask, "What's wrong? Don't you feel well?"

If this is true, why can't the opposite also work? You get up in the morning, and you don't feel well. How difficult would it be to tell yourself, "You know what? I don't feel well, but I know that if I act as if I do, I'll feel better."

I used to work with a man that, if I wanted to, I could talk into not feeling well. One day I said, "Hey, Josh! What's wrong?"

"Nothing; why?" But he began to look alarmed.

"I don't know," I continued, "but you don't look like you feel well."

"Really?"

By lunch he'd be gone.

Our communication style with ourselves and with those around us helps us maintain control over our minds and care for others in the process. I use a four-letter acronym, SOFT, to help me remember this.

SOFT: S Is for Smile

I often ask people, "Can you hear a smile on the telephone?" Surprisingly, they say, "Yes," and I understand why. Smiling changes our intonation. It changes the way we say things and the way we sound. It changes the way we feel when we are talking to others. The simple act of smiling, relaxing some facial muscles, turns our faces into instruments of helpfulness.

My younger daughter used to say, "Dad, a smile is just a face echo." When I smile at people, they tend to smile back, returning that face echo back to its sender. So smile. It doesn't cost you a thing, and it increases the value of your mind. It helps your mind convince yourself and your body to say, "You know what? It's a good day. Things are going pretty well." Smile. It's one of the best stress-reducers on the planet. Smile. Smiling is not only good for the carrier; it's a benefit for those who receive it.

SOFT: O IS FOR OPEN

Be open. What does that mean? If you walk into someone's office and see a person sitting behind the desk, who is in charge? That's right; he is. It's his office. It's his desk. Furniture is utilitarian—we spread our work out on it—but the placement of it reflects a mind motive. If we sit behind a desk that is placed in the center of an office, we say to all those who enter, "Hey, I'm in charge." If we turn that desk around so that we are on the same side, and we turn around with a big smile, shake a person's hand, and say, "Hi; how are you?" all of a sudden there's no one in charge. Our mind motive is using furniture to actually set the stage for who's the boss. So tell me: Do we mind our mind? Be open.

Many hotels have figured this out. Instead of walking up to an imposing front desk, you walk up to a small pedestal check-in station. The person standing beside it talks to you and makes you feel as though you are in charge.

The real lesson in this, though, I have learned by going into other people's offices. I've been in the offices of some very influential people. Every time I enter one of these offices I ask myself, "I wonder what their furniture is going to tell me about them."

Not too long ago as I sat in the waiting area of an executive's office I kept trying to visualize what his office would look like. Since he ran a rather large corporation, I thought, *Big desk. Powerful desk.* And I was right—it was 12 feet long, mahogany, hand-carved, and absolutely gorgeous. But I was a little shocked to see that the desk was not in the center of the office. It was pushed over along the wall near a window that looked out over the city. The only thing in the center of that office was a couch and two chairs. Not even a coffee table.

He was cordial in his greeting but seemed to realize that the furniture had thrown me off. And then this man asked me the pivotal question: "Dale, did you come here to see my furniture, or did you come here to see me?"

Good question. At every opportunity, get as few pieces of furniture as possible between those you serve and yourself. Tell your mind that your job is to serve. The most powerful leaders in the world will tell you that they are servants. And their furniture will tell you what they are thinking.

SOFT: F Is for Forward

Lean forward. Simply lean forward. I stole this part of the SOFT acronym from my wife. Debra was a kindergarten teacher. I remember visiting her classroom and watching small children come over and tug on her skirt. My wife would turn around, lean forward into the child's face, and say, "What is it, sweetheart?"

Do you know the difference between a kindergarten student and an adult? None! (Well, maybe between 18 and 30 inches.) We are the same person. We have the same brain. We react and respond positively to others who react and respond to us in a positive way. Leaning forward is that kind of action. When we are talking to someone, we rarely stand with both feet exactly square with the person to whom we are talking. Most of the time I have one foot in front of the other. I do that for a reason: if I place one foot in front of the other, I put the weight of my body on the foot closest to the individual talking to me. This causes me to lean forward, and lets the person know that they are important to me. This action, the body posturing of taking your physical self and aiming it at the person to whom you are talking, causes your mind to listen.

Perhaps you've been to one of those workshops that try to help us remember the names of people when we first meet them. I guarantee that if you lean forward and genuinely listen, you will remember people's names.

Do you know what it's called when two people get together and interact with each other for 30 minutes, both parties understanding every single word and intention of that exchange? No, it's not called communication—it's called a miracle. That's because most times while you are talking to me, I'm thinking about what I am going to say next. And while I am talking to you, you're thinking about what you are going to say next. We rarely actively communicate with one another—because of our minds.

Smile. Be open. Lean forward.

I am the Sam Walton of communications. That's going to take some explaining. In his many travels, as he was building his Wal-Mart empire, Sam Walton said that he always found brilliance whenever he visited a competitor's store. Maybe they weren't selling as many items as they would like, or maybe they weren't as prosperous as they would like to be, but Walton always found some piece of brilliance that he could take back to Wal-Mart that would help his employees.

I walked into a Wal-Mart in Tupelo, Mississippi, early one morning. Over the loudspeaker I heard, "Give me a W!"

From all over the store came the response, "W!"

"Give me an A!"

"A!"

"Give me an L!"

"L!"

"Now, feel it! Give me an M, A, R, and T!"

With a great deal of excitement these people completed the Wal-Mart cheer.

As I checked out my items at the front of the store I asked a smiling clerk, "Doesn't that get a little old every morning? I mean, come on. The Wal-Mart cheer?"

She laughed. "Well, for one moment in time every person in this store is focused on one thing: our customer, and making that customer's experience at Wal-Mart a positive one."

I'd say she was minding her mind. Or maybe she had figured out how to make her mind mind *her*.

SOFT: T Is for Touch

The T in the SOFT acronym is a little hard to sell. Did you know we already live in a touchless society? We've so actively removed touch that we've almost eradicated it from our communication style. We've let people tell us that it's not appropriate. We've had a few people tell us that they don't want to be touched, so we enter that information into our brains and apply it to everybody else. Don't do that!

When the iron curtain came down in Russia, we got a good look at some of the orphanages there in that country and the alarming rate at which some of those children, small infants, were dying. It wasn't that there was inappropriate nourishment. These infants were dying because they had no one touching them.

Touch is a powerful thing. When a small child is threatened, what do they do? Well, they grab a leg. I can't tell you how many times a child I don't know has grabbed my leg for comfort. Now, if they look up and see that their dad's face isn't above the other end of that leg, it takes a small amount of processing time before they think, *H'mmm. This isn't my dad, but I'm not going to let go of this leg until I can find another one to grab on to.*

Touch is powerful. Nevertheless, few people have our permission to touch us. Aside from our family, close friends, doctors, nurses, dentists, dental hygienists, massage therapy people, or cosmetologists, the list is pretty small. If we're not careful, we will become a touchless society, desensitizing ourselves to the power and the miraculous healing nature of touch.

Because of the inability of most of us to accept the power of touch, I like to talk about it in what I call three doses. We'll start with the dose I refer to as the "business" touch—shaking hands. Why do we shake hands? Well, it's a timing mechanism. We shake hands to time the experience. Further analysis has caused me to divide the handshake into four separate experiences—the single pumper, the double pumper, the wiggler, and the dead fish.

You know the single pumper. You walk up, one pump, they're done.

The double pumper is similar to the single pumper, only they give two pumps instead of one.

The wiggler wiggles. They don't really pump; they just make a small jerking motion. These people tend to be longer-touching people, more friendly. And that wiggling motion enables them to hang on a little bit longer.

And then there's what I like to call the dead fish. I don't think I have to explain that handshake—all you get is the fin, the end of the fingers. This one really bothers me. I tend to just wiggle right upstream and grab as much of the hand as I can.

Handshaking is about timing. I was a wiggler for many years. Then several years ago I was standing outside the Palms Restaurant, where I was going to have lunch with a good friend. Because of some scheduling problem he was unable to be there, and I was going to have to eat lunch by myself. Here I was, at one of the nicest restaurants in Washington, D.C., by myself. I don't like to eat by myself. Food digests better when you're looking into another person's face.

I made up my mind in that instant that I wasn't going to eat by myself. I would wait by the door until someone came in by himself, and ask him to eat with me. You will never believe who walked into the Palms Restaurant: Senator Tip O'Neill. I practice the SOFT formula, with one small caveat. I believe that if, during the first 30 seconds of interaction with any individual, you can make them laugh, they will remember you. I boldly walked up to Tip O'Neill, extended my hand, and said, "Mr. O'Neill, my name is Dale Henry, and I am from Kingston, Tennessee. Do you know how many times I have seen you sleep on television?"

Tip O'Neill had an infectious laugh. When he laughed, his whole body laughed. Then he did something I will never forget. He didn't shake my hand; he greeted me. As I moved toward him and extended my hand the senator didn't extend his. Instead, he held his hand close to his body, palm up. It caused me to have to walk in a little bit closer and place my hand in his hand, and he had big hands. He didn't squeeze, he didn't wiggle, he didn't shake, he didn't pump. He was perfectly still.

I really can't tell you how long we stood there. It could have been 10 seconds; it could have been 10 minutes. I really don't know, because I lost track of time. He smiled (he was extremely open), and he leaned forward. "Mr. Henry, Kingston, Tennessee? Kingston, Tennessee? That's in east Tennessee, isn't it?"

"That's right, Mr. O'Neill."

"How blessed you are."

These days if you meet me and give me permission to be in charge during our greeting, you will get a Tip O'Neill handshake. I will hold my hand close to my body, and I will cause you to have to come in a bit closer. I'll smile at you, I'll be open, I'll lean forward, and, most important, you'll get a touch. You will get a greeting. You and I will share an experience that hopefully will help you remember me. It will tell you the motive of my mind, which is to get to know you.

This isn't something that comes naturally to any of us, and it wasn't natural for me. But it has become as natural to me as breathing, because I told my mind that's what I want to do. I've learned how to control some of the things I do. I'll never be in full control probably, because the mind is a pretty powerful thing. If we will start to understand its power, though, we can make it a learning mind.

I told you that the touching part of the SOFT formula comes in three doses. The first dose is, of course, that business greeting—the handshake, the greeting we use from day to day as we go about our jobs. It's an appropriate thing, but by being still, we make it different. By smiling we make it different. By being open we make it different. Leaning forward causes us—and those with whom we are talking—to be better communicators.

The second dose is the friend's greeting. Friends don't deserve a handshake; they deserve a hug. Men should hug men. Women should hug women. Men should hug women, and women should hug men. The Bible tells us to greet each other with a holy kiss. I can already feel your mind taking control. This gets back to the motive part of the mind. As long as your mind is pure, then what you do is pure as well.

Here's the test. If you do anything for your own motives, they are wrong. But when you do something to help others, how can it be anything but right? Hug one another. Especially those who are close friends. During that brief moment that you are hugging, your mouth and your friend's ear are so close that it gives you a chance to say, "Hey, thanks for being my friend. Thanks for being there when I needed you. Thanks for being here for me." Hug friends.

I'm an equal opportunity hugger. To tell the truth, I almost prefer to hug men more than women. Men tend to be pretty good huggers. Women give what I call tent hugs: tops close, bottoms far away. People who know me well know that I'm a hugger, and they know that they aren't going to get away without one.

A good friend of mine, Leonard Davis, in Louisville, Kentucky, will probably testify to this. We meet each other in airports many times during the year, and we always give each other a loving and brotherly hug. If you were to walk by and see Leonard and me greeting each other that way, it would look a little strange: Leonard is more than six feet tall, and I am five feet six. But you know what? It makes us feel good, because we know our minds' motive. It's to be there for each other—to be a friend.

The third dose, or level, of touching is for those you love—your family. Your family definitely does not deserve a greeting. Your family definitely does not deserve a hug. Your family deserves to be *embraced*. Most people don't understand the difference. It's pretty simple.

A hug is when you put your arms around someone, pat them on the back, and tell them how much you appreciate them.

An embrace is when you take hold of someone you love and, as you are holding them, talk to them. If this interaction doesn't last longer than 45 seconds to a minute, then it's too short. Embrace them and tell them how special they are to you. Make that touch mean something more than simply a touch. Implant information into that person's brain that they are important to you, vitally important to you. The touch is an implanter of information. Let me give you two examples.

When I would visit my grandfather's home, 99.9 percent of the time he would place his hand on my shoulder and say, "Son, it's good to have you here. You're home now. Thanks for coming. We love you." After I'd had that done several hundred times, my grandfather could literally walk over and place his hand on my shoulder, and without his saying a word my mind would hear: "Thanks for coming. You're at home, and we love you." Without making a verbal sound, he communicated those things to me with just a touch.

I love to cook. Sometimes when I'm cooking, my wife will come up behind me, wrap her arms around me, lay her head on the back of my neck, and just stand there. Let me tell you what Debra is saying: "I love you, honey. I'm sure glad you're cooking. If you need me, I'm going to be downstairs in the recliner." How do I know that's what she's thinking? Because I've heard her say it. By merely touching me, she communicates to me exactly what she's thinking.

The SOFT formula is pretty powerful. For me to tell you that nothing's ever going to backfire on you when you use it would not be the truth. I'll tell you some of the things I have read that make this whole formula work for me. One is the fact that I once read in *Psychology Today* that if you don't get five hugs a day, you could be seriously weird. I don't want to be seriously weird, so I usually end up soliciting hugs on the road. They feel good.

It has backfired on me. Once in Tupelo, Mississippi, I was doing a program for an industrial group of employees, supervisors, and managers. (It was the same time that I first heard the Wal-Mart cheer.) At the end of the program I looked toward the back of the room, which had been filled with 500 people. There stood a man who looked a little like Grizzly Adams. A big guy. No, he was a massive guy. I would say he was about six feet six and weighed more than 350 pounds. (I'm five feet six and weigh 150 on a good day.)

I walked up to this man, who was now the only one left in the room. When I extended my hand to greet him, he pushed it away, reached down, grabbed me by my waist, and picked me up. Now I'm looking at him eyeball-to-eyeball, feet dangling in the air. In a strong Southern drawl he said, "You know how long it's been since I've hugged another man?"

That's not the kind of question you answer in Tupelo, Mississippi. I thought it best to offer a noncommittal "Umm?" in a very shrill voice that told him I was out of breath.

He set me down then and said, "Dr. Henry, I didn't even want to come to this program today. My boss made me come. But as you went through the SOFT formula, I understood what you meant when you said the mind has motive. I remember thinking to myself this morning when I got up that I didn't feel good. I had pretty much convinced my body, through my mind, that I wasn't going to have a good day. I really had no desire to be at this workshop. But as you went through this method of how our minds, through proper ways of thinking, could control the way we act, and that we could care for one another, my mind began to open.

"When you got to the T in the SOFT formula, my heart almost broke. Do you know how long it has been since I have hugged my son, Dr. Henry? More than 30 years. When I leave this auditorium today, I am driving down to Jackson, Mississippi, where I am going to hug my son."

I felt sorry for his son. I had know this man for only two hours in a workshop, and he gave me a hug that I will never forget. I was thinking that his son was going to need chiropractic help. But the motive would be right. It would be an experience that both he and his son would remember for a long time.

I like to try to envision that experience. I try to envision that he smiled, that he was open, that he leaned forward, and that he and his son touched, embraced. I like to think SOFT. That's how we need to be with one another—soft. However, the motives of our minds will not always allow us to be soft. The motives of our minds and the self-talk that we have with others sometimes control our expectations, and creativity and action are driven by a hopeful mind-set.

Conversely, how the mind is conditioned when individuals believe themselves worthless and expect to fail causes a whole inability to recognize positive, helpful information. If not checked, it will lead to total ineffectiveness and selfishness. The mind can sometimes be conniving, adventurous. It can cause us to have wrong motives, to twist the truth. In some instances we do things we would not do under normal situations. Let me tell you a story I first heard in church as a small boy. Maybe in some minute way it will illustrate how our minds are able to make us do things.

Once upon a time there was a man who was a carpenter. This man became very good at his craft, a master carpenter. As his reputation grew, more and more people began to trust his work. Not only trust it, but admire it. He became known as the best carpenter in town. Unfortunately, being very good at something doesn't always make a person wealthy. And that was the case with this man. He had worked his entire life in a very serving way.

One morning at breakfast his wife planted a seed in his head. She asked him if he had given any thought to retirement. Like most people who love what they do, retirement wasn't something he had thought about. But the seed that had been placed in his mind began to grow and twisted the way he saw himself. On the way to work that morning he started thinking: *You know, I don't have that much to show for my successes. Oh, I can look around this town and see the beautiful homes that I have crafted and the appreciation of those for whom I have worked. Obviously, because I stay very busy I'm able to provide jobs for others, too. But I am not rich. I should be rich.*

This carpenter, this craftsman, had started to let his mind have the wrong motive. He was letting his mind be conniving. When we allow our minds to be conniving, we start to live too much in ourselves. This is what he was doing. This was his plot: *I've got to make more money. People trust me. They admire me, and I need to start think-ing about me more.*

Big mistake. That afternoon he went to the work site where he had several homes under construction. One of the richest men in town approached the master craftsman. He said, "Do you know how much you are admired in this town?"

Not thinking with a pure motive, he didn't hear that. He corre-lated admiration with being a servant. He was thinking of being sub-servient. That's when it happened. That's when his mind conceived the thought.

The rich man continued. "I want you to build me a home. I bought a tract of land on top of the mountain, and I want you to build for me the most beautiful home in town. Price is no object. I want the finest of materials, and I want your fine crew, the men whom this town admires as master builders, to build this home. I'm going to be out of the country, doing some extensive traveling, and I won't be back for four months. Would it be possible for you to have the home completed at the end of that time frame?"

Of course, the builder said, "Yes." He thought, *Here's my chance to make some money, a chance to build my own prosperity.* And he put his plan into action. He didn't buy the finest materials. He bought substandard and charged for the finest. He didn't use his best crafts-men. And whatever mistakes were made, they were plastered and painted over. All the things that were done wrong were not seen.

Four months went by, and the project was completed. The rich man pulled up in front of the house, and as was customary for the master builder, he showed the man through his new home. He talked about the details. He talked about the special care that had been taken, knowing in his heart that it wasn't so. He talked about craftsmanship, but he knew it was substandard. Walking to the door of that mansion, the craftsman laid the keys in the hand of the rich man and said, "Welcome to your home."

A huge smile spread across the rich man's face. He put the keys back into the builder's hands and said, "My friend, you have been a giver to our community, a man who has been faithful, never caring once for his own gain but only watching out for the good of others. No, my friend, this is not my home—this is yours."

We live a lifetime, you and I, and those things that we do, those things that we complete, will be our legacy. Our mind will help us to do the right thing only if we learn how to control it, only if we learn to be compassionate, only if we are caring. When we become careless, when we place ourselves first, we will not be happy.

8

Individualize Your Influence

Keeping your failure rate low: Sustaining momentum with a glass that's half full.

He who loves a pure heart and whose speech is gracious will have the king for his friend.—PROVERBS 22:11.

When you ask someone how they are, they'll usually respond, "Fine," "OK," "Tolerable." I have a friend who answers that question by saying, "You know, things aren't half bad."

He's exactly right. Things happen to us every day that aren't half good, but the others aren't half bad. Human nature almost dictates that in a half-bad, half-good world we concentrate on the bad, not the good. My philosophy has always been "Expect the best." I find that when I expect the best, I usually get it. When I expect the best, my mind will do that very thing—expect the best.

In this chapter we'll look at the contrast between optimism and pessimism. We'll see how the positive thinker isolates undesirable events, viewing the bad as temporary and taking partial credit for good results.

When we expect good and believe good things will happen to those who expect them to happen, our bodies do an interesting thing. If you are walking in a dark alley or a parking lot or parking garage, and you are sure someone is following you, chances are you feel a little stressed. Maybe your heart beats a little faster, and you feel an anxiety inside. What you experience is the body trying to protect itself. It's a natural occurrence.

When we worry about things, we cause the body to go to a place like that parking garage. We imagine what's going to happen, and our body puts that anxious, stressful feeling on us again. In a half-half world, you are now living in the bad half. I can't do that, and I don't want you to do that. I want you to expect the best. Let me show you what I mean.

A couple years ago the phone rang in my office. A pleasant young woman on the other end said, "Dr. Henry, how are you doing?"

"I'm doing absolutely wonderful!" I responded. "Thank you for asking. And yourself?"

"Blessed."

I don't hear that response very often, but I liked it a lot. "How can I help you?"

"Dr. Henry, I'm a meeting planner. I'm having a conference for 3,500 administrators, and I'm looking for a speaker."

"Great! Sounds like my kind of program. When is your conference?"

"Friday."

"Ma'am, this is Tuesday."

"That's right."

"And you're looking for a speaker for a conference on Friday?"

"That's right."

"Wow!" I said. "You really get things together in a hurry! I mean, it's kind of unusual to be looking on Tuesday for a speaker for a conference for 3,500 people on Friday."

"It's like this," she explained. "The speaker we really wanted couldn't come."

Now I felt better! "That's OK. I'm so honored that you thought of me next."

"Well, actually, you are the eighth person we've called."

By now any pride I may have had was pretty well gone. "Well, no need to call anymore," I told her. "I'm open on Friday, but unfortunately, I'll be out of the office until Thursday morning. So any information you want me to look at will have to get to me by Thursday morning when I get back to the office."

"No problem," she said. "I'll send out a package to you."

My busy week brought me home Thursday morning. My wife handed me a package and said, "This arrived for you yesterday." Tearing open the package and dumping the contents out on the table, I noticed something that I guess you might say took me by surprise—a first-class ticket.

Don't get me wrong. I like first class. I ride in it occasionally when I take long trips from the East Coast to the West Coast. The reason it surprised me and made me think *Expect the best* was that I hadn't asked for a first-class ticket. It's simply not the responsibility of my clients to fly me first class. Being a smaller person, I find first class nice but not a necessity. For bigger or taller people, first class is probably an option they'd like to have, one they'd tend to expect. In this situation, however, it was totally uncalled-for. Still, I saw it as an expect-the-best and the-glass-is-half-full experience.

I grabbed up all the information and headed for the airport. Once on the plane, I began to look through the material. On the outside of an envelope was this note: "We'll have someone there to pick you up at the airport." How nice! Expect the best! Sure enough, when I stepped off the plane, there was a young man who was wearing a black cap, black bow tie, and black jacket. He was holding up a small chalkboard on which he had written "Dr. Henry." I walked up and introduced myself.

"Dr. Henry, is this your luggage?" he asked.

"Yes, it is."

He grabbed my suitcase and headed for the door. This isn't the first time this has happened. Actually, it happens on a regular basis; however, the person picking me up is usually a hotel employee waiting at the curb in a hotel van.

That's what I was expecting to happen that day. After all, some good things had already happened. I got a first-class ticket. (That's nice. That's a half-full experience.) Someone had picked me up at the airport. (That's very nice. When you're in a strange city, you know how much more relaxed that makes you.)

But there was no hotel van at the curb. At the curb sat a big black stretch limousine. Everybody who has ever seen a stretch limousine always thinks, *I wonder who's in there?* I knew people would be thinking that, so when I got in I rolled the windows down and started waving at people. The interesting thing about being in a limousine and waving at people is that they wave back. We stopped at the corner near the airport exit. Two older women bent down and peered in. "He looks bigger on TV, doesn't he?"

I just knew the hotel was going to be another expect-the-best experience. And I wasn't disappointed. It was a gorgeous hotel, absolutely beautiful! I walked into the lobby, waving goodbye to my limousine driver as I made my way to the front desk. And at that point the smallest bit of my euphoria evaporated.

Have you ever dealt with someone who had a snooty attitude? Well, the woman behind the front desk had a snooty attitude. Turning one shoulder into me, she said, "May I help you?"

I said, "Yes, ma'am. My name is Dale Henry. I believe I have a reservation here."

"Well, we are just going to have to check, aren't we?" she said.

"That's fine," I said, determined not to let this woman's attitude affect which side of the glass I was looking through. Still half full, I waited and smiled.

What happened next was only short of a miracle—this woman experienced an amazing transformation right before my eyes. She went from being one of the snootiest people I had ever met to being my best friend. "Oh, Dr. Henry," she cooed. "What an honor and privilege it is to have you at our property."

Obviously she knew something that I didn't.

She began pecking on the computer again, and the next thing I knew, she held her hand over her head and started snapping her fingers. Folks, it was like roaches at midnight. People appeared from every crevice of that hotel and swarmed around me like bees to honey.

I said, "You know what, folks, I'm low maintenance. I don't need a lot of help. I don't have a whole lot of luggage. I kind of like taking care of myself, but I sure do appreciate it."

As quickly as they came, they disappeared. My newfound friend behind the counter held out the plastic key that would let me into my room. I grabbed the key and started to put it in the lapel pocket of my coat.

"Oh, no, Dr. Henry!" she cried. "Please wait. I've got something just for you." She laid a metal key on the counter.

That's when I knew what was happening. If you have a Southern accent like mine, you lose about 50 points of intelligence for every time zone you travel through on your way to the West Coast. It's as though there's a sign over your head that says "goober." I figured my goober buzzer must be going off, but, determined not to allow my glass to become half empty, I smiled.

Many people don't understand what I call "the goober phenomenon." This phenomenon occurs because of CNN, the Cable News Network, which is based in Atlanta, Georgia. On a slow news day they'll send out a crew to somewhere like Macon or Athens, Georgia, to cover a tornado. They interview somebody during that presentation and, for some reason, it always turns out to be the same person—a guy with one tooth that he licks when he talks, wearing a baseball cap twisted to one side. The interview goes something like this:

"Sir, what happened to you during this horrible tragedy?"

"Well," he answers in a heavy Southern drawl, "you're not a-gonna believe this. I's settin' in my trailer watchin' rasslin', and somethin' come up in my yard, makin' a turrible racket. It grabbed a-holt of my trailer and shook it 'round with me inside, like shakin' a box with a puppy. Next thing I know, the windows is breakin'. My wife, Mabel, flew right off the commode, out the bathroom window . . . Mabel darlin', if you're out there, come home, 'cause I'm hungry." (During the entire conversation our friend from the

South licks his tooth. Why in the world is he doing that? Because he's got only one left—he's trying to keep it clean; he's proud of it.)

Whenever you hear that on television, you turn to the person next to you, wherever you live in this wonderful country of ours—except in the South—and you say this: "You know, every one of them is just like that."

Voilà! The goober phenomenon. I have witnessed the goober phenomenon before, and I figured this metal key was just in case I was too stupid to know how to use the plastic one. I snatched it up and got into the elevator, which was packed with people from the conference who were going to their rooms.

Pressing against the wall, I asked the man next to the buttons if he would mind pushing my floor. He said, "Not at all. What floor are you on?"

"Twenty-five," I said.

He giggled. "Somebody's pulling your leg [read "goober"]. This elevator doesn't go to the twenty-fifth floor, because there are only 24 floors in the hotel."

"Well, my key says 2501," I said.

"Then you must have to walk that last flight of stairs."

A woman wearing a housekeeper's uniform reached through the crowd from the back of the elevator and grabbed hold of my jacket. Giving it a nice light tug, she asked, "Sir, did they give you a key?"

"Yes, they did."

"Then you're in the suite!"

Imagine that. I was in the suite! So I inserted my metal key in the elevator's keypad, and up we soared. Stepping off on the twenty-fifth floor, I understood why I was the only one who got off—there were only two rooms up there, 2501 and 2502. As I approached 2501, double doors—beautiful, ornate, carved doors—swept upward from the floor to the ceiling. I inserted my plastic key, and they opened before me. It probably didn't happen, but I swear I could hear "The hills are alive with the sound of music."

The room was so big that I had to give it the east Tennessee test for largeness—an east Tennessee yell. Sure enough, an echo came back. The room was that big. In the center of the room stood the bed. In the South we push our beds up against a wall so nobody can sneak up on us. I had never slept in a bed in the center of a room. I lay there all night, looking over my shoulder.

Then I saw another set of double doors. I had never been in a hotel room that had two sets of doors. Wondering if that was part of my room too, I opened those double doors, and there was an entertainment suite, complete with big-screen TV and a pool table.

That wasn't the end of it. There was another massive room. The drawing room, and I hadn't even brought any crayons.

To be honest, the only room in that suite that I felt comfortable in was the bathroom, except that it had a phone in there. I don't answer the telephone in the bathroom, because you have to overcome that first question: "What are you doing?"

I walked out of the bathroom and called my wife. "Debra, I wish you were here; this is a gorgeous room!"

She instructed me to go immediately to Wal-Mart, buy a throwaway camera, and take lots of pictures. Do you know what would happen if I ran downstairs, jumped into my limousine, and shouted to my driver, "Hey, run me down to Wal-Mart, will you?" They would have thrown me out of that place on my ear. Instead I went down to the hotel gift shop. This gift shop had throwaway cameras. Unfortunately they were those underwater type; but I got some great shots from the tub.

And that's when my glass started looking empty. I was standing in that room and having a conversation with myself. "This can't be my room. This can't possibly be the room that I'm supposed to be in. There's been a mistake. There's another Dr. Henry, and I'm in his room."

I'd had this kind of room mix-up before at a conference in Albuquerque, New Mexico, when I stayed at the Embassy Suites. I had stayed in Embassy Suites before—they are all basically the same.

When I arrived at the conference, the meeting planner asked, "Hey, how do you like your room?"

"Oh, the room is great."

I didn't think much about it. An hour later she came over and said, "I bet you really liked that room, huh?"

Which started me thinking. *Well, all rooms are the same, but maybe she thinks I'm a goober, and I'm not used to staying in hotel rooms this nice.* So I complimented the room again, saying, "The room is lovely."

At lunch that afternoon I got the same question. "Are you enjoying your room?" And that night at dinner and the next morning at breakfast: "How's the room?" During the two days that I was there she must have asked me about that room 10 times. And every time, in a pleasant voice, I said, "Yes, I love it."

At the end of the conference a very embarrassed meeting planner approached me. "You must think I am so silly. I've been bugging you about this room for the past two days, and I just realized that your two-room suite was given to one of our attendees whose last name was also Henry."

It happens. That's why I began to think, *This beautiful suite can't be mine.* About then someone knocked at the door. My brain shrieked, *See? Here they are to tell you that you're in the wrong room.* Standing outside the door was a young man dressed even better than my limousine driver. He extended his hand and said, "Dr. Henry, my name is Melvin, and I am your valet."

We stood there for a few moments, discussing the beauty of this gorgeous hotel. He told me that the vice president of the United States had stayed in room 2501 two days earlier. That set my brain to whirling. Who must be in the *other* room across the hall from me, the only other room on the twenty-fifth floor?

That's when the elevator door opened. Stepping through the elevator door was a man I recognized immediately: Zig Ziglar. I leaned into Melvin and said, "Melvin! Strangest thing, but that looks just like Zig Ziglar."

"Dr. Henry, that *is* Mr. Ziglar."

"What on earth is Zig Ziglar doing here?" I asked.

Melvin looked surprised. "You don't know? Mr. Ziglar is

speaking tomorrow from 10:00 to 12:00. You're speaking from 1:00 to 3:00."

This was not good news. "Melvin, what would be the chance of getting some Pepto-Bismol?" He thought I was kidding. We stood there a few more moments and discussed some things about the hotel that I didn't know.

Melvin said, "Now, Dr. Henry, when you go out of your room to go eat dinner tonight, make sure you flip the switch that's by your nightstand that says 'valet.' That will tell me that you aren't in your room, and I'll come in and prepare your room for the evening."

I had never had my room prepared for the evening.

He continued, "I don't want you to unpack your clothes— please allow me to do that for you."

That sounded good to me. I went back inside, my head still spinning from the thought that Zig Ziglar would be speaking at the same conference as I. All of a sudden I heard a knock at the door. Thinking that Melvin was already back with the Pepto-Bismol, I opened the door—to Zig Ziglar, his hand extended.

"Hi, my name is—"

"I know who you are," I interrupted, bowing at the waist. "And I am not worthy."

We laughed, and he said, "Dr. Henry, I was wondering if you would like to go out and eat dinner."

And we did. What a wonderful, charming Christian man. Coming back to my room later that evening, I opened my door and saw that my bed had been turned down. I have never had my bed turned down before. You may have had your bed turned down, but was it ironed? Melvin had ironed my bed. It was too pretty to get in. On the pillow was a quarter pound of fine German chocolate, not one of those itsy-bitsy chocolates.

Have you ever tried to sleep after eating a quarter pound of chocolate? When I woke up the next morning, all the covers and pillows were on the floor. Looking around the room, I began to wonder where my clothes might be. There were several large closets,

so I began looking through them. Finally I found my two suits and
white shirts, freshly pressed and covered with little tissue bags bear-
ing the hotel monogram. On the floor my extra pair of shoes had
been polished until they gleamed, and sported little freshener inserts
in each shoe. *Obviously he smelled them,* I thought glumly.

One of the reasons this goober phenomenon exists is that people think we Southerners are slow. We're not slow. We do, however, ponder. I was standing at the door of my closet, pondering. I
lived at home for 19 years. I had a wonderful mother and a great
father, and they took care of me exceptionally well. But you know
what? They had never put little freshener inserts into my shoes. Dad
had never ironed my clothes and covered them with a tissue bag
with a monogram on it. I've been married to a wonderful woman
for 27 years—my child bride, I like to call her. But in 27 years she
had never done that for me either. I started thinking that if anything
ever happened to my wife, valet service was looking pretty good.

Then I began to wonder where my underwear might be. I looked
through the hundreds of drawers in that huge bedroom and finally
found them. To my amazement, Melvin had ironed my underwear,
too. He didn't just iron it; he rolled each piece into a roll and slid a
little ring over it. They were the prettiest things I had ever seen.

This whole experience was an expect-the-best experience. It
sounds perfect, doesn't it?

But it wasn't. Did I tell you that my flight was delayed? that I
got sick? that a piece of my luggage got lost? No, I didn't. The reason is that I didn't see the experience that way. My glass was half full,
and everything that happened to me filled that glass a little fuller.

Sometimes people want to live in a half-empty situation. What
a shame to live in a time frame where stress lives. As Casey would
say: "That ain't my style." I believe that this whole attitude I have
keeps my failure rate low. It helps me sustain momentum because
my glass, well, it's a little bit more than half full. You could pretty
much say it "runneth over."

▀▄ ▀▄ ▀▄ ▀▄ ▀▄ ▀▄ ▀▄ ▀▄ ▀▄ ▀▄ ▀▄ ▀▄ ▀▄ ▀▄ ▀▄

9

Individualize Your Worth

Building a relationship with your value by checking the foundation for flaws.

Do you see a man skilled in his work? He will serve before kings; he will not serve before obscure men.
—PROVERBS 22:29.

My wife has retired from teaching now, but I remember the yearly ritual of asking her what she was going to do on her summer break. One time she said, "This summer I think I'll come and work for you in your office."

I love my wife. I love being with her and sharing time with her. I'm just not sure that I want to be in business with her, because business has nothing to do with love. I love Debra, but unfortunately I know her habits. If you are married, you know that the last thing you do is reveal the way you feel about a situation by the way you look at your wife.

I somehow managed to put a smile on my face and say, "Hey, that would be great!" I also knew my wife well enough to know that she would probably change her mind. Sure enough, the first week of summer break she said, "You know, honey, it's been a while since I've seen my mother in Little Rock, Arkansas. I think I'll go and see her for a couple of days."

Every woman reading this book knows that two days means two weeks.

I said, "Honey, I think that's a great idea."

Two weeks later she called me from Little Rock and said, "You know, it's been a while since I've seen my sister in South Carolina. I think I'll go and see her for a couple of days."

Deep in the recesses of my mind I was thinking, *Great. A couple more sisters and two more relatives, and Debra will be gone all summer.* I had a big conference in California that my staff had to attend with me, so no one would be in the office.

When we returned, we expected Debra would still be gone on her vacation. So when I grabbed the doorknob and the door opened by itself, it sort of took my breath away. It was Debra, wearing a huge smile. "You're never going to guess what I did today!" she bubbled. "I went to work in your office."

That was scary, but I managed to squeak, "What did you do?"

"Oh, I answered phone calls . . . But the really cool thing is that I booked you for a program!"

That brought me back to full voice in a hurry. "Debra, you can't book me for a program, because you don't have my calendar."

"That's the best part! I don't have your speaking calendar, but I know your 'off' calendar. So I just put you to work on a day that you would have been off."

That was pretty smart, I thought. "Tell me a little bit about this program," I said.

"It's great! It's going to be in Nashville, Tennessee."

Nashville is less than a two-hour drive for me. That's a good deal.

Debra continued. "It's going to be in Nashville at the Maxwell House. It's going to be for 350 salespeople, and it's going to be a luncheon. Honey, the great thing about this is that you can leave in the morning, do the program, and be back in time to eat dinner with us that night."

She was right. It was a great plan. I said, "You know, honey, since this is the first time you have ever done this, you might want to let me touch base with the client and find out if there's anything you might have forgotten."

"Oh, I didn't forget anything," Debra assured me. "I talked to this guy for almost two hours. I know everything about the program."

"Honey, I'm sure you think you know everything about the program, but since you've never done this before, there are obviously some things you might have forgotten."

Her whole countenance changed. She went from excited and thrilled to very hurt. She threw the paperwork down on the table and said, "Well, there it is. Call him if you want to hurt my feelings."

After 27 years of marriage I knew what that meant: "Make that phone call, and you'll be eating peanut butter and jelly sandwiches and sleeping on the couch for a couple of days."

So I said, "Honey, you know what? I trust you. I believe you have done an excellent job, and I'm not going to call my client. I think you have the situation in hand."

A big smile crossed her face, we had dinner together, and it was a good day.

Several weeks later I was getting ready to go do my program. I don't know what you do on a weekend day; I'm very busy. I have two daughters, and I love to watch them play soccer. I have never played soccer, but that doesn't keep me from coaching. That's one of the reasons my girls sometimes don't like it when their dad shows up. This day I was determined to keep my tongue in my mouth and have a good day.

After being there for an hour or so, I realized that I had to head for Nashville. I kissed my wife, waved goodbye to my girls, and went home, changed clothes, and drove to Nashville. When I was about halfway there it occurred to me that I hadn't eaten all day. If you're little and skinny like me and miss a meal, you might just die. So I started thinking seriously about finding a place to eat.

And that's when I remembered that Debra had told me that this program was a luncheon. I'd grab something at the luncheon. Quite often at banquets and luncheons I'm served a French dish called Chicken Robert. If you don't know French, allow me to translate. It means rubber chicken.

I arrived in Nashville early. (I pride myself on being early.) I got out of my car and strolled slowly to the front of the Maxwell House. There was a man pacing back and forth on the front step. All of us know body language well enough to know that people pace when they are anxious or upset. People pace when they are burdened. Then he looked at his watch. *OK*, I thought, *he's anxious and impatient about the time, and he's worried.*

That's when I realized that of all the details my wife had gotten exactly correct on this program she had booked, the only thing she had erred on was the time. Debra knew there was an hour's difference in time between where we lived and Nashville, Tennessee. Unfortunately, she got it backwards. I was now 30 minutes late.

I ran to the front door, almost colliding with the man's jabbing finger. "I hope you are Dr. Henry!"

"Sir, I am indeed."

"I've got good news for you."

Of course, I'm thinking he's going to say, "You're 30 minutes late, so you might as well jump back in your car and go home." Instead he smiled and said, "The power has been out in Nashville for 45 minutes. You're right on time!"

We walked into the banquet room, where he seated me at the head table. I was really hungry by now, so hungry that my belly button was rubbing against my backbone. When you sit down at a table with people you don't know, what do they want to do? Talk!

The man to my right looked over and said, "Dr. Henry, I am indeed looking forward to your presentation today. May I ask you a personal question?"

"Of course you can," I said.

"Would you mind sharing with me what you love most about your job?"

"That's easy," I smiled. "What I love about my job is looking into other people's faces when I do what I do."

When he heard this he got the strangest expression on his face. "Really?"

"Yeah."

He stopped talking to me. I am from Harriman, Tennessee. In my little town you can talk all day about practically nothing. But I was thinking, *You know what? This guy's like me. He's hungry. He wants to eat.* So I started to eat my chicken.

Before I had a chance to take a bite, the man on my left said, "Dr. Henry, I've read several of your articles."

I used to be the dean of a college. I have written hundreds of articles. But when somebody actually finds one, that makes you feel good. "Really!" I responded, interested.

"Yes, I have."

"Would you mind telling me which article you liked best?"

"I liked that article you wrote on technique. That is one of the finest articles I think I have ever read."

Feeling warm all over, I said, "Well, you know what? Technique is one of my favorite things to write about."

"What is your favorite technique, Dr. Henry?"

I held my hand up straight, with one finger pointing toward the ceiling. "I love to give it to Them."

The strangest look came over his face, and he said, "Really?"

I said, "Yeah."

He quit talking to me too.

Let's recap. I had been at this program for five minutes. One man is obviously upset with me for being late. Two men sitting at the head table aren't talking to me, and I don't have a clue why. To be honest with you, I was hungry and really didn't care.

So I finished my meal, placed my napkin on my plate, and looked down the head table. I caught the eye of a man at the end of the head table. He gave me a wink. I thought it must be customary, so I winked back.

He stood up and walked across the stage and around the lectern until he was next to me. He placed his hand on my shoulder, looked deep into my eyes, and said, "Outside of the fact that you are a well-known proctologist, how would you like me to introduce you to the audience?"

I nearly swallowed my rubber chicken whole. "Excuse me, but I could have sworn that you said proctologist."

"I did."

"But I'm not a proctologist. I don't do that."

"What do you mean, you're not a proctologist?"

"I mean I'm not a proctologist! I don't practice proctology."

"You're not Dr. Michael Henry?"

I held my hand up in a time-out sign. "Whoa, whoa, whoa! That's the problem! My name is Dale Henry, and I am from Harriman, Tennessee."

He put both hands to his face in the unmistakable international signal of distress. "Then there has been a terrible mistake!"

Right-hand guy and left-hand guy sighed. "Well, what a relief!" one of them said. "Because any proctologist who does their job while looking into people's faces is doing it differently than we do!"

The other one added, "And a proctologist who likes 'to give it' to people has a different technique from ours."

This is a funny story. We could stop right here and go on talking about our worth. But as Paul Harvey says, now you've got to hear the rest of the story. Two meeting rooms down at the Maxwell House in Nashville, Tennessee, Dr. Michael Henry was getting ready to do his presentation in front of 350 salespeople. The kicker was that he had slides! In every one of our heads lives an evil twin. When our evil twin sees something like this, it says to us, "You know, you ought to just let this go and see what happens."

But I couldn't do that to another speaker. So I walked up to Dr. Henry and said, "Your name is Dr. Michael Henry, is that correct?"

"It is," he said.

"And you are a proctologist from Memphis?"

"Yes," he said.

"Dr. Henry, this is a group of salespeople."

He scratched his head. "Sir, you will not believe my luncheon conversation."

"Well," I said, "I think I've got a pretty good handle on that."

We moved Dr. Henry and his slide projector to his audience of proctologists.

Just for a second let's pretend. Let's go to that place that only humor can take us. Let's use our imagination and consider what would have happened if I hadn't stopped Dr. Michael Henry.

I can just see him standing in front of the audience of salespeople. Although I've never seen him speak, I can imagine his program would begin something like this: "Ladies and gentlemen, to get you from where you are today to where you would like to be tomorrow is very simple. All you have to do is this, right here."

I can imagine Dr. Henry pointing the clicker for the first slide, and every salesperson in the audience shaking his or her head, declaring, "No, no! I don't care what it pays; I'm not doing *that* for my customer."

Our biggest asset in understanding our own worth is our sense of humor, our ability to laugh when the unplanned, the unexpected, happens. I love my sense of humor. Sometimes I laugh for my own entertainment, and sometimes I think of things that entertain no one but me. I like to laugh.

We have to laugh. They say that a 3- to 5-year-old child laughs about 300 times a day. Children find things to laugh at that an adult would never consider funny: the dust coming through the window, a dog licking their face—anything gives them an excuse to laugh.

Adults laugh barely 20 times a day. That's a shame. Laughter is a good sign of good self-esteem, of good self-worth. That's not the only sign, though. By itself, liking to laugh does not give me self-worth, but it's a good start.

My daughters and I are close. I'm amazed at how many times I learn lessons from them. LeAnne and I were going out to get a video and pizza, which is one of our special things we like to do when we have family time in the evening. As we pulled onto the road that goes to the local Pizza Hut, coming directly toward us was a funeral procession. I have always been taught to pull over out of respect for those who have lost a loved one, and that's what we did.

Sitting there by the side of the road, my daughter said, "Wow, Dad! That person must have been rich."

It occurred to me that she and I had seen the same hearse drive by, and it wasn't pulling a U-Haul. So why would she say that person must have been rich?

I asked her what she meant.

"Dad, that person had a lot of friends."

Friends make us rich. Friends add richness and self-worth and value to our lives. I have had two such friends who have done that for me. Both of these men, in very separate ways, have enriched my life and improved its worth. Let me tell you their stories.

Steve Reagan and I were childhood friends. We played together. You never saw one of us without the other. We were very close. Then when we were in the seventh grade, Steve's father got a job in another town, and they moved away.

I mourned the loss much as one would mourn a death. I missed my friend. But time has a way of healing all wounds, and before long I had forgotten my friend Steve. I went to high school, got married, and went to college.

During my sophomore year I received a phone call one Sunday afternoon. "Is this the Dale Henry who once lived in Maryville, Tennessee?"

I said, "Yes."

"Is your mother's name Mae Bell? Is your father's name Alfred?"

"Yes."

"Did you go to Allenwich Elementary School?"

Finally I demanded, "Who is this?"

"Dale, it's Steve."

"Steve! How are you? It's so good to talk to you, my friend! Can we get together? Let's have lunch or maybe meet at the library and spend some time talking."

We agreed to do that. I need to tell you that my childhood friend Steve was a rather large individual. Not that that's important, but it's important at this part of the story. Steve was also a redhead, so it wasn't going to be hard to pick him out. As I sat at the University of Tennessee's graduate library waiting on my friend, I watched every person who came through the door, looking for a heavyset redheaded man.

When a thin redheaded man with a very nicely trimmed beard came in, I immediately said to myself, *That can't be my friend Steve.* But it was. Steve saw me and started to smile. I haven't changed that much since grade school, nor have I grown that much. We embraced and talked for a few minutes. I told him how good it was to see him and how good it felt to be in his company once again.

After lunch we continued to sit at the table for an hour or so of more conversation. Then Steve looked at me and with a big smile said, "Not exactly what you expected, was I?"

I played dumb. "What do you mean?"

"Oh, come on, Dale! Admit it. You were looking for a fat redheaded guy, weren't you?"

"Well, I'll have to admit, that did cross my mind."

He laughed and said, "Would you like to hear my story?"

I was thinking that his story had something to do with some weight-loss plan or some program he was on. But what I heard next has changed my life.

"Dale, do you remember 1972?"

"Of course I do, Steve. Nineteen-seventy-two is the year you and I graduated from high school."

"Exactly," he said. "You would have known me then, Dale, because when I was practicing for graduation I weighed about 400 pounds. When I came out of that graduation practice, I sat on the front fender of a friend's truck. He was going to run me down to my car, which was parked in the parking lot. You know how boys are, Dale. He goosed the car, and I leaned back on the hood, afraid I was going to fall off the truck; then he hit his brakes. That threw me headfirst into the grill of another automobile, and I was in a coma for almost four months.

"Dale, when I woke up, it was like waking up from a night's

sleep. My mother was standing at the foot of my bed, crying. I said, 'Mom, what's wrong?' She wiped her eyes and with amazement said, 'Steve, you've been in a coma for four months.' I didn't believe her. She said, 'Look under the covers.' When I did, Dale, I was gone. For the first time in my life I could actually see my feet."

That's a pretty powerful story, but I didn't really hear it. Oh, I heard the story. I listened in amazement as my friend told me all the events that had taken place in his life. But I missed the point, the moral, the proverb. I missed the part of the story that would have made me the prize. But as God does, on occasion, He gave me another chance. He gave me the story in a different version with the same theme.

In 1991 I was finishing my doctoral work at the University of Southern Mississippi. During that time I had made another lifelong friend, Greg Little. Greg and I became very close for several reasons. We have a lot in common, we like to laugh, and we had a lot of classes together.

But the reasons aren't important. What is important is that we were good friends. One day he said, "Dale, do you know why you are one of my good friends? Do you know why you are one of my best friends?"

"Well, Greg, I would assume it's because we share many things in common."

"Oh, that's true," Greg agreed. "But one of the reasons we are very good friends is that you've never once noticed that I flutter." This malady is a little like stuttering but is manifested in a slightly different way.

But that's not important to the story. What is important is that I told Greg, "You are my friend. When someone is my friend, acquaintance, or coworker, I try my best not to think of any disability or weakness they may have. Rather, I try to look at their strengths. I look at the things they do amazingly well."

"Nevertheless, Dale, I would like to tell you my story. In 1972 I was graduating from high school. Driving home in my car one day,

I had a wreck, and I went into a coma. When I woke up from that coma, I had to start my life over again. I had loved music, but had forgotten it. I didn't know the people who loved me. I didn't recognize them. I had to learn how to talk, walk, and feed and dress myself. It was bad, but I did wake up."

Immediately after that conversation I tried to connect the parallels of my two friends' lives. There were many common areas, but the message I think God wanted me to get was the one most of us would miss, the one I missed. Here is the most important thing my friends had in common: both of my friends *woke up*. They didn't waste their lives; they got on with them.

It is amazing to live in a country that is so full of blessings, so full of opportunity, so full of reasons to celebrate every day of life, and yet to see people who are miserable living it. Our worth to ourselves and to others is measured in several different ways. It's measured by how much happiness we bring to one another by lifting each other up. It's measured by the fact that every day we do wake up and live and love and serve one another.

There is another lesson that, again, a friend has taught me. While at the University of Southern Mississippi I fell in love with gerontology, the study of the older adult. I love the more "experienced" adult! I want to tell you about Carl. Carl is 82 years old and has had a lot of experience. Carl is a good friend; God has blessed me with Carl. He is an individual who is always there if you need him. He is helpful, kind, gentle—all those things we normally associate with worth.

I told him once, "Carl, you sure do laugh a lot."

"Dale," he answered, "it's because folks my age have no peer pressure. All the ones who were worrying have died."

An interesting way of putting life into perspective. Carl's real gift, though, the thing that Carl does for me personally, makes him my prize. Carl is a prayer warrior. I don't know where he gets his information about me, but Carl is like an old guided missile. When he finds out that you have something going on in your life that he thinks can be helped by prayer, he'll hunt you down.

Carl found out that my sister-in-law, Pam, an intensive-care pe-
diatric nurse, had hurt her arm during an accident. "Dale," he said
in his scratchy old voice, "I understand your sister-in-law's not feeling well." He asked if I would like him to intercede with a prayer.

"That would be absolutely wonderful," I said.

He reached into his pocket and pulled out a three-ring binder so
old that it was being held together with duct tape. Turning to a clean
page, he pulled out a small pencil barely long enough to write with,
licked the tip, and said, "What's her name, Dale?"

"Her name is Pam."

"P-a-m, Pam. Last name?"

"Field, Carl."

"F-i-e-l-d. Is that with or without an s?" Carl asked.

"No s, Carl."

"Middle initial?"

"Carl, her middle initial is A."

"A. Does that stand for anything, Dale?"

"Yes, Carl, it stands for Ann."

"Ann. That's important. A-n-n. Is that with or without an e?"

"No e, Carl."

"Singular Ann. Now, let me read that back to you, Dale. It's
Pam Ann Field."

"Well, actually, Carl, it's Pamela."

"That's important," Carl said. "Where does she live, Dale?"

"Little Rock, Arkansas."

"L-i-t-t-l-e R-o-c-k, Little Rock. What's the zip code there,
Dale?"

Confused, I said, "Carl, does God need a zip code?"

That didn't merit an answer. "Zip code, Dale?"

"I don't know the zip code, Carl."

"OK. I'll look it up. Street address?"

"106 Sheffield Drive."

"1-0-6 Sheffield. Oh, look, that's cute! Sheffield—Pam Field.
Drive, D-r-i-v-e. Now, let me read this back to you, Dale. It's

Pamela Ann Field, 106 Sheffield Drive, Little Rock, Arkansas. I'm going to look up the zip code."

I said, "Carl, thanks so much for being my friend."

He said, "Dale, don't be in such a hurry. You young people are always in a hurry. What's wrong with her?"

"It's her arm."

"Arm. A-r-m. Is that the left arm or the right arm?"

"Left arm, Carl."

"L-e-f-t a-r-m; left arm. Is that above the elbow, below the elbow, or at the elbow?"

"It's at the elbow."

"Elbow; e-l-b-o-w. What kind of pain is it, Dale?"

By now I'm thinking, *The kind of pain you're becoming, Carl,* but I didn't say it. "It's a shooting pain."

"S-h-o-o-t-i-n-g p-a-i-n; shooting pain. Now, let me read all this back to you and make sure I've got all the facts and data correct. It's Pamela Ann Field, 106 Sheffield Drive, Little Rock, Arkansas; Carl's going to look up the zip code. It's her arm, her left arm, pain's at the elbow, and it's a shooting pain. Have I got it, Dale?"

My relief was palpable. "Carl, I can safely tell you that you now know everything I know." He closed his little notebook, put it back in its place in the lapel pocket of his coat, and stuck the pencil in his shirt pocket.

He started to walk away, but I called out to him. "No, no, Carl; you're the one in a hurry now. I travel around the country, speaking to audiences, and do you know what my main goal is, Carl? My goal in speaking to an audience is to try to implant into their minds a passion—a passion to be the best they can be. The only way they can live an optimum life is to be passionate about that life and passionate about everything they do. Carl, you have that passion. You have a passion about being specific in prayer. Why is that, Carl?"

He seemed almost surprised. "Dale, you've got to be specific, because God is busy. If I didn't tell God your sister-in-law's name, where she lived, and what was wrong with her, He'd have to look around. He ain't got that kind of time, Dale."

I said, "I understand your reason for specificity in prayer. But what I asked you was why you have a passion for it."

He hung his head. "Oh, that. You didn't know me when I was 58 years old. I wish you had known me then. I was a good-looking man. I had a full head of hair. I was a babe magnet. Between the ages of 58 and 62—that's when it happened."

"That's when what happened, Carl?"

"That's when I started to pray. When I was 62 years old I woke up one morning, looked into the mirror, and all my hair had fallen out. With the comb in my hand I looked at myself and I thought, *Hey, all of them have jumped ship. There's not any reason to give a couple of them any extra attention.*

"But that's the day I started being specific in my prayer. I looked up that morning and I prayed, 'God, give me hair.' Dale, hair has grown out of my ears and on my ears. My eyebrows have become incredibly bushy, and I have those big black hairs coming out of my nose. And only the good Lord knows where this hairy spot on my back has come from.

"But not one single solitary hair has ever grown on the top of my head. And do you know why, Dale? Because you have got to be specific!"

So let's be specific. How do we get worth in this life? It's really very easy. Life has no predictability. There's no guarantee that either you or I will be here tomorrow. We have this day, this beautiful day, that the Lord has made, and we are to be glad in it. You can't be of worth to yourself or to others unless you are glad. Have a good sense of humor, laugh, enjoy life, and wake up every day and live it.

But don't just wake up yourself. Wake up those around you as well. Though we have no choice about whom we work with or whom we are around every day, we can choose to make this a good day. Be specific in your prayer. Don't make prayer a ritual. Make it a conversation with your Savior. Thank Him every day for the bread you get to eat, the ground you get to walk on, and the air you get to breathe, because they are gifts.

A gift is not something that you work for or deserve. A gift is something someone gives you because they love you. And to be loved gives us self-worth. We love one another, and through this love we begin to review the changes that have occurred as we mature, and to consider how these changes will affect our subsequent behavior.

We see how independence, imagination, and trust are built through laughing and learning. We see how our lives have been heavily influenced not only by our own youth and the youth of others but by the youthful ideals of the more experienced adult.

Individualize your own worth, and then you will begin to build a relationship with your value by checking the foundation for flaws.

S E C T I O N

4

ZING!

10

Zing Others With Your Ability to Plan

Mentoring: Giving others a leg up before it's the only one they have to stand on.

To search out a matter is the glory of kings.
—**PROVERBS 25:2.**

Growing up, I wasn't what you would call a Rhodes scholar. I wasn't the best student in the class, and I definitely didn't have the highest GPA. There was, however, one particular teacher who made a difference in my life. Mr. Skidmore was my shop teacher.

There is no telling how many shop teachers have turned kids' lives around. Mr. Skidmore did that for me. He taught me how to work with wood and how to draw plans. But the thing that really stands out in my head is that Mr. Skidmore taught me to plan ahead. He taught me to think about a particular project before I undertook it. He made me look out there into the future and see it.

I can still hear Mr. Skidmore: "Dale, before you build it, try to see it. Try to place in your head the image of what you're going to build. Once you have it there, draw up your plan and proceed with your plan of action." Another way of putting it might have been "Dale, you need to take *aim* on your problem."

AIM is a great acronym, especially when it comes to developing mentorees. Now, if there is any area that I know quite a lot about, it's how the brain works. Oh, not the scientific method—I have my

own way of putting it. I believe that inside our head live two people. One person is a computer programmer. He sits up there and at
1,100 words per minute types in information that comes in through
the many sensory devices the body uses. Eleven hundred words per
minute! That's phenomenal. That's how quickly the brain works.

Now, I said there were two people. The second person of this
pair is Goober. Goober's job is to wait for the computer programmer's shift to end. Then with one finger he mashes a button that
reads "print." All the information the computer programmer has put
on your hard drive for that day is downloaded onto sheets of paper.
Goober stacks the paper very neatly, puts it into boxes, and stores it
in the attic of your brain. Right about now you're thinking, *This is
pretty ridiculous,* but let me prove my theory.

Let's say you're grocery shopping. You see someone you know
as well as yourself. You know their name, where they live, what
they do for a living. You say, "There's, uh, that's uh . . . Oh, I know
his name as well as my own . . . Don't tell me! It's on the tip of my
tongue." But for the life of you, you can't remember that person's
name. What you've just done is put Goober in action. You've told
Goober you want that person's name. Goober then runs to the attic
of your mind and, one sheet of paper at a time, he's looking for this
person's name. Later, you're asleep for the night. It's 2:00 in the
morning when you sit straight up in bed and say, "It was John!"
Goober has just come through for you.

The mind works a lot like that. You know as well as I do that
there are not really two little people in your head. But these two
functions of the brain are really just about that simple. At 1,100
words per minute the hard drive of your brain sits up there, whirling
and gathering information that comes through your eyes, ears, nose,
fingers, and all the sensory mechanisms your body has in its control.
Collecting information isn't the only thing the brain does. It also
takes and stores the information and has to get it withdrawn. That's
where Goober comes in.

AIM: A IS FOR ASSESSMENT

The AIM method is a lot like these two mechanisms in the brain. Every day, no matter what happens in your life, you have to make an assessment. You have to look at the day and say, "OK, what is my primary goal? What things would I like to achieve today? Whom would I like to help?

Chances are, the majority of us don't go through this exercise. We get up, get a glass of juice, and head to work. Wherever we stopped the day before, that's where we take up our schedule again, never once asking, "How can I more effectively do today what I learned yesterday?"

Do the proper assessment. Whom can I help? What can I do? How can I do it better? Where do I need to be? What time do I need to be there? A plan of action.

AIM: I IS FOR INNOVATION

Be different. Do things differently.

We have homogenized ourselves. We drive the same cars. We dress the same way. Whatever fits the norm, that's what most of us do. There's not a person on this planet who would like to be introduced in this way: "This is my friend George. And you know what? George is just like everybody else." Not very flattering, is it?

Try this one on for size: "This is my friend George. He's a unique individual. He has a wonderful personality, but, all in all, he's one of the most different people I know. He is very, very unusual." Anyone would find this introduction very intriguing and flattering.

The main idea of innovation is not only to be different but also to think differently. Most of us think in terms of being a mentor. Not me. I look at this whole process as one of finding mentorees, people who need to be helped. Not everybody needs help. Not everybody will take it. But finding mentorees who will take guidance, people whom you can help, is indeed planning ahead.

AIM: M Is for Motivation

Motivation is a very misunderstood word. Nearly everyone believes that motivation is something someone else does for you. It's not. Motivation is something you must do for yourself. It's an action that requires some stimulus, and that's where the AIM formula comes into play.

Let me show you how this works. In your head is a brain that's about the size of your fist with the other hand laid on top. I know you were hoping for something a little larger, but that's basically the size. Your hand on the top of your fist represents the portion of the brain that I call the hard drive—the storage mechanism.

Now look at your fist. This represents the part of the brain that does everything on its own. You should be happy. Because of this, you don't have to think about breathing. You don't have to think about food processing or waste removal. You don't have to think about repairing cells. The body does all this on its own through this central mechanism of the brain over which we have no control.

Look at your wrist. This represents the brain stem, the most primitive part of your brain. Although we have no control over it, we do see how it is controlled. In an earlier chapter we talked about the nervousness, that stimulus of an apprehension sensation, that we feel when we're walking in a parking garage at night. The brain stem controls that. It's the gatekeeper; it lets everything in. It's what funnels the 1,100 words per minute of information into your brain.

Now we know about the AIM method—assessment, innovation, motivation. We know how the brain works. We know that the top part of the brain is the hard drive, and that the middle part of the brain takes care of every one of your body's needs without you having to do anything. And we know that the brain stem, the most important—and the simplest—part of the brain, is the gatekeeper.

Most of us don't believe we are as smart as we really are. We've heard that we use only 10 percent of our brain, so we're pretty satisfied with that. God gave you a tremendous device that can be used in a variety of ways, not only for your own success but also to study, memorize, and become smarter. One of the reasons God gave us this amazing ability was so we could help others—mentoring them.

One of the world's best archers is from Clarksville, Tennessee, not far from where I live. He can do marvelous things with a bow and arrow, but I'll guarantee that he didn't just wake up one morning, step out on the back porch, and say, "Well, I think I'll squeeze off a couple arrows into that grapefruit a hundred yards away." Everything he did for success had to be thought out to the last detail, even measuring the humidity in the air. That long stretch of time from pulling the bow to hitting the target is affected by even small amounts of moisture.

Let's take each step of the AIM formula, and see how it can help us to meet our objectives by doing an assessment. Here we go! Can you name the first 10 presidents of the United States? You can probably come up with several of them, but chances are you don't know all 10. This is a little perplexing, because you've seen pictures of them hundreds of times. The first 10 presidents of the United States represent information, knowledge.

We all know stuff. You know that if you eat your fruits and vegetables, you will be healthier. If you exercise 30 minutes a day, you'll have more energy. You also know that if you get eight hours of sleep each night, you'll feel better, and you'll do your job more effectively. You know these things, but do you do all of these things every day? You have only knowledge—you haven't learned anything yet. Learning is the ability to apply what we know.

Let's apply what we know by doing a little exercise. Imagine you're sitting in a room with your back against one wall. You look around and see four corners, four walls, a floor, and a ceiling—10 areas of the room to help you remember the first 10 presidents of the United States. To apply what you know, the two things you must do are look where I tell you to look and see what I tell you to see. Then you must practice this one time before this time tomorrow. Here are your instructions:

We'll work our way around the room, starting at the front

right-hand corner of the room, as you're facing it. Imagine that in that corner is an old-fashioned washing machine with the wringer on the top, rocking back and forth. The soap suds are bubbling out of that washing machine and falling onto the floor. *Place the washing machine in that front right-hand corner—number one.*

On the wall to your right you to see an atomic bomb with a big mushroom-shaped cloud. All that energy, that massive amount of explosive power, has been released by that atomic bomb and is being exploded on that wall. *The atomic bomb is on the wall to your right— number two.*

Put a very large chef in the back right-hand corner. He's a big guy, massive. And he's got on his white coat and his big poufy hat. Standing next to him is his small son. They're holding hands and getting ready to cook together, because they both have on poufy hats, and they both have on white coats. *Chef and son are standing in the back right-hand corner—number three.*

Now, let's review. Flipping back to the corner on the front right-hand side, you see a washing machine. On the right-hand wall you see an atomic bomb. And in the back right-hand corner behind you stand the chef and son.

Now look at the wall you're leaning against, the wall in back of you. On that wall place an old-time drugstore, maybe like the drug-store in the town where you lived as a child. Look through the plate-glass window at all the medicine. See the Alka-Seltzer and the aspirin? *The old-time drugstore is on the wall directly behind you—number four.*

In the left-hand corner of the wall behind you is an ATM ma-chine. This ATM machine has gone crazy. Money is rolling out of the machine and piling up on the floor. Stacks and stacks of money are rolling from the ATM machine. *Put all that money in the left-hand corner of the wall behind you—number five.*

On the wall to your left is a huge mirror. If you look in the mir-ror, you'll see a reflection of the atomic bomb that is on the wall to your right (number two). *The mirror that reflects the atomic bomb is on the wall to your left—number six.*

Someone has placed a car jack in the front left-hand corner. They've jacked up that corner, and you can see right underneath that corner into the next room. *The front left-hand corner contains a car jack that lifts up the corner so you can see the next room—number seven.*

Let's review again:

In the front right-hand corner, number one, is the old-time washing machine.

On the right-hand wall, number two, is an atomic bomb.

In the right-hand corner behind you, number three, are the chef and son.

A drugstore with all that medicine in the window is on the wall directly behind you, number four.

In the left-hand corner behind you, number five, is the ATM machine with money rolling out.

A huge mirror on the wall to your left reflects the atomic bomb, number six.

In the front left-hand corner, number seven, is a huge car jack, which allows you to see underneath and into the next room.

Someone didn't set the parking brake on a moving van, and it has crashed through the wall in front of you. You can see the nose of the van poking through. *The moving van coming through the wall in front of you—number eight.*

The carpet on the floor is really hairy, growing up between your toes. *The hairy carpet—number nine.*

Look up at the ceiling. There are square things called ceiling tiles up there. *The ceiling tiles—number ten.*

Review time again! If you will look over to the front right-hand corner, number one, you'll see an old-time washing machine.

The right wall, number two, has an atomic bomb.

In back right-hand corner, number three, are a chef and son.

On the wall behind you, number four, is a drugstore with lots of medicine.

The back left-hand corner has an ATM machine with money rolling out, number five.

Number six, on the left wall, is a mirror showing nothing but the reflection of the atomic bomb, which is on the right wall.

In the front left-hand corner, number seven, is a car jack, jacking up the corner of the room so that you can see into the next room.

In front of you, someone didn't set the parking brake, and the nose of a moving van has crashed through the wall.

Of course, down under your feet is a hairy carpet, number nine; and over your head, on the ceiling, are tiles, number ten. Now, I have a question for you. What do you know?

"Well, nothing more than a bunch of useless information," you say.

Exactly. People you will meet, people you will mentor, will have lots of information. Unfortunately, they aren't using it. That's what finding the right mentoree is all about—helping them use the information that they already know.

We are so smart. We know so much good stuff. But we never use it, because we never use it in its application. You think that what you know is a bunch of useless information. Let me tell you that what is going to happen next is kind of neat. I am going to review for you two times the first 10 presidents of the United States. Then I'm going to ask you to close your eyes and name them for me. I can already hear your self-doubt. I can already hear you say, "Oh, I can't do that." Sure you can. It's so simple. It's so easy. You are so intelligent and so smart. Here we go!

In corner one, of course, we have Mr. Washington—the washing machine. On wall number two is Mr. Adams—the atomic bomb. Back in corner three, Mr. Jefferson—chef and son. On the back wall is Mr. Madison—all that medicine from the drugstore. In the back left-hand corner, number five, is Mr. Monroe—all that money rolling out of the ATM. On the left-hand wall the huge mirror has nothing but a reflection of the atomic bomb—and that is Mr. Adams (the son of the first Mr. Adams). In the front left-hand corner is a car jack. Of course that's Mr. Jackson. In front of us is Mr. Van Buren, the moving van. Underneath our feet is Mr. Harrison, and the ceiling is Mr. Tyler.

I would like to review them one more time. No pictures this time, just the presidents. Here they are: Washington, Adams, Jefferson, Madison, Monroe, Adams, Jackson, Van Buren, Harrison, and Tyler.

It's your turn now. Lay down the book, review the first 10 presidents, and marvel at the power of the AIM formula. You're probably going to want to know where the M comes in, the motivation part. No one has ever been motivated to do anything. Motivation comes from within yourself. If you are motivated, if you have the proper motivation of wanting to mentor other people and have them be your mentoree, then you are motivated from success—the ability to do something well. That's our motivator. Most of us get frustrated because we don't do things well, and we have to do them again and again. This anxiety over making errors constantly cannot lead to successful thinking.

Let me give you an example. I am an only child—no brothers or sisters. I had to be kind of imaginative. I married a woman who has four sisters. At this time none of them are married, so that makes me surrogate husband to four other women. This is a pretty good position to be in, especially since all of these women live in other states. I love to talk to them on the phone. They call me all the time, asking me for information.

Until now I've been able to think that I'm pretty smart. I'm not really very good at fixing things, but I've made them believe that I am. Pam, Debra's oldest sister, called not long ago. She said, "Dale, my car is making a strange noise."

"Really, Pam? What is it doing?"

"Every time I stop, it goes eek-eek, eek-eek."

"H'mmm. When does it do that, Pam?"

"When I stop."

"You know what, Pam? That sounds like brakes to me."

"You think so?"

"Yeah, I do. Why don't you run it over to one of those brake places, and have them take a look at it?"

"Oh, you are so smart, Dale!"

Well, of course I am. I live somewhere else. Because I live somewhere else, I am an expert. All of that changed when one of my wife's sisters decided to go to the University of Tennessee. She is close now, and I am not the expert I was when she lived farther away.

Not long ago her sink clogged up, and she called me at the house. "Dale, my sink is stopped up," she said.

"No problem. Just pour some Drāno down the sink, and that will take care of it."

"I already tried that," Cindy said. "It didn't work."

I didn't say anything, but in my mind I was thinking, *Ooh, that's all I know.* I said, "Cindy, you know what? Dad and I are going to Knoxville tomorrow. We'll run by and fix your sink."

She said, "OK."

I hung up the phone and called my dad. (The only person on this planet who knows less about fixing things than I do is my dad.) I said, "Dad, tomorrow while we are in Knoxville, we have to go by Cindy's and fix her sink."

"No problem," he said. "We'll run by Wal-Mart and pick up some Drāno."

"Dad, she's already tried that."

"Ooh," he said. "That's all I know."

"I know, Dad. You taught me. We can't go over there looking like we don't know what we're doing. We've got to have a plan of action."

"You know what?" Dad said. "Down the street a new neighbor moved in, and I believe he's a plumber. I'll run down there and see what he would recommend. I'll call you back."

An hour later my dad called and said, "Pick me up tomorrow. I've got our problem all solved."

As I pulled up in his driveway the next day, Dad was standing on the curb with what looked like a hubcap under his arm. As he got in the car I asked him what he had. He said it was a snake. It didn't look like a snake.

"What does it do?" I asked.

He pulled out a wire with a small attachment on the end. "All we have to do is stick this down the sink, twist it, and it will unclog the sink."

On our way to Cindy's we devised a plan. Our plan was to get Cindy out of the house. If she was in there, she'd watch us, and we didn't want that to happen. So when we got there we said, "Cindy, all we really need is for you to run and get some more Drāno. We're going to fix the clog with the snake, but we'll need some Drāno to put down in there to flush out the system."

She said, "I'll go right now."

That left Dad and me alone to work the snake, a device neither of us had ever seen before. We both agreed it would be best to get on top of the sink, with a straight eyeshot into the hole of the drain. It was definitely a job for two. Dad was going to unroll the snake, and I was going to stick it down in the hole and twist it.

Many of you might not know this, but a man believes that if a little bit of something is good, a lot is even better. This was a 75-foot snake. Before we knew it, we had more than 50 feet of snake stuck down into the drain, pushing and twisting, pushing and twisting. Finally, after giving the snake a push, I felt like I had hit the bottom. I could almost hear it: *thud-thud, thud-thud.* I turned to Dad and said, "I wonder what that means, Dad?"

"It's the end of the line, son. Give it a twist and bring it in."

So I twisted and twisted and twisted the snake and started to pull it up. As I pulled it up, Dad was wiping it off and rolling it up, cleaning off the tool, as both he and I like to do. After pulling up about nine feet of the snake, I felt it snag. It wouldn't pull up any farther, and I couldn't get it to move.

"Dad, what do you think has happened?"

"Well, I don't know, but I do know we can't just cut it off and poke it down into the sink. Son, we borrowed a 75-foot snake. We've got to take back a 75-foot snake. I'll bet when you twisted it that last time, you put a kink in it. Why don't you push it back down and twist it in the opposite direction? The kink should come out."

That made sense, so that's what I did. I pushed it back down, gave it a huge spin in the other direction, and started to pull it up. After coming up nine feet, it snagged again in the same place.

"You know what, son?" Dad said. "If you had some pliers, some channel locks, so that we could grab hold of this wire, that might do the trick. I'll bet the problem is that it's too slippery, and you can't pull it past that section. Maybe it's an elbow or something."

"Dad, you know, you're right." And I walked down the steps of Cindy's apartment to the ground floor. I saw a young woman with two small children peering into the door of the apartment. Finding this a little strange, I approached the woman and asked, "What seems to be the problem?"

She turned to me with the strangest look on her face and said, "Mister, we were sitting at the kitchen table having our breakfast when this thing came out of the sink. It grabbed hold of the rug in front of my counter and started spinning it around. Then it pulled the rug into the sink. When I got up to see what was happening, it spit it back out again. Then it twisted the rug in the other direction and pulled it back up into my sink. It wouldn't have been so bad, but we just saw that movie *Alien.*"

Surprised and embarrassed, I admitted, "You know, I might know a little bit about that."

She grabbed me by the arm. "Be careful!"

I walked into her kitchen and saw the snake sticking out of her sink and into a small rug at the front of her cabinet. It had tangled itself all up. Releasing the rug from its grasp, I stuck the snake back into the drain. By the time I got upstairs, Dad was frantically rolling the snake up into its container, and we made a hasty retreat.

Those things we do best, those things at which we excel, will be the things that we will help those around us accomplish best. So many times we have fallen into the trap of thinking that practice makes perfect. It does not. Practice merely makes permanent. If you don't get better, you are just going to get the same old thing.

As a small boy I wanted to be a baseball player. Oh, I practiced!

I threw pitch after pitch after pitch. I found a place at the back of one of my grandfather's sheds and threw baseballs until my arm hurt. Let me tell you, I got good. I could throw a fastball that would make your hand sting, and accuracy wasn't a problem. But I had learned only one pitch.

I had heard that a Babe Ruth League team was trying out at the park in downtown Maryville, so I went over to try out. Of course, it was me—and a couple hundred other boys. When the coach asked, "Who wants to pitch?" about half the group moved to the left. Boy after boy got up on the mound.

Finally it was my turn. As I stepped onto the mound, I visualized that basket I had been throwing fastballs through all those times behind my grandfather's shed. And that's where I threw it. I had practiced until I could absolutely hit that mark. And I could do it not only with accuracy but also with a great deal of speed. It gave me a lot of pleasure to watch the catcher have to take off his glove and rub the palm of his hand against his jeans.

The coach stepped up to the fence, wrapped his fingers around the chain links, and shouted at me on the pitcher's mound. "Son, let me see your curveball."

Curveball? I had no clue what a curveball was, but I twisted my hand around and threw a couple of other pitches. He wanted to see a slider, a change-up. I constantly changed the way I threw the ball but to be honest, it was a fastball.

The coach came out to the mound, placed one foot on the mound, and said, "Son, I'd like for you to pitch for me."

I didn't need ground to walk on. I could have flown all the way home.

Then he said, "When you get home, I want you to practice your fastball."

I said, "Coach, my fastball is my best pitch."

"No, son, your fastball is your only pitch."

Don't practice the things you don't do well. Practice the things you do extremely well. God has given you a talent, a gift. Use it! He has also given you the talent to be able to take your gift and show others how to apply it in their lives. Use your gifts for the good of others! Recognize the gifts and strengths that come from mentoring those around you. Develop the tolerance and steadfastness that comes from planning ahead, zinging those around you not only with your ability to plan but with your ability to aim with integrity.

11

Zing Others With Your Level of Commitment to Service

The hootie-hoo attitude: How to make the buck stop here and have a real good time!

He who gives to the poor will lack nothing.
—PROVERBS 28:27.

I had the opportunity to work as a salesman at Miller's department store while I was going through college. I liked being of service to my customers, and I liked helping people. On occasion that joy would be stretched.

One evening a woman came into the store shortly before closing. She wanted to look at men's suits, and I showed her everything in the store. Unfortunately, she bought nothing. My sales manager was closing out the cash register when my customer left. I told him there was only one thing I disliked about working there—the motto of our store.

He looked at me with some confusion. "Motto? What would that be?"

"It's the one we use here all the time," I said. "You know—the customer is always right."

That night my manager straightened me out. He told me that even though that might be the philosophy of the store, every good salesperson knows that the customer isn't always right. So he revised that old motto for me in a completely different way. Unfortunately,

I didn't hear it. Perhaps it was my youth. Perhaps it was the fact that I was aggravated and wasn't ready to learn.

Many years later I was in Washington, D.C., to speak to the organization that maintains all the Internet data for the military. Because we had planned this presentation at the last minute, my travel plans weren't what you would call ideal. We had a four-hour layover. My secretary, who was with me, suggested, "You know, we could go shopping."

During my 27 years of marriage I'd heard that one once or twice. It seems like when there's any time, it's always time for shopping. Like Bill Cosby says about Jell-O, there's always room for it. I didn't want to go shopping. Mainly because I knew from experience that any time a woman wants to go shopping, she doesn't mean run in and get shoes and leave, or run in and get a sweater and leave. She wants to see every one in the store. I did not want to spend four hours walking around looking.

When I was a young boy, my mom took me to the Dollar General store and bought me two pairs of jeans, two shirts, underwear, socks, and one pair of shoes. I thought that's what everybody's mother did. As I got older I discovered that other people had more than I did. That didn't seem fair. My mom and dad loved me as much as those other kids' parents loved them. So why did they have more? This thought formed in my young mind: I may never have a big house. I may never drive a fine automobile. I may never have a lot of money. However, I decided I was going to have shoes. I've got more shoes than that Marcos lady in the Philippines. I love shoes!

My secretary knew this. She said, "You know, I'll bet they have shoes there."

"Let's go shopping," I said.

Making the transition from the Dollar General store to such places as Dillard's was a massive jump. But the jump I was getting ready to make this day made that leap look like a small hop. You see, the first store we went into at Tysons Corner, near Washington, D.C., was Neiman Marcus. As we entered through the men's clothing department I spotted a silk handkerchief. I stuck it into my jacket to see how it looked. It was very complementary to the outfit I was wearing.

"Oh, you should get it," my secretary said.

I looked at the price tag and knew it was time for me to move on. It cost more than my suit. I told her I'd meet her outside in the mall, where I was going to find somewhere comfortable to sit and pursue my hobby of watching people.

On my way out I walked through the men's shoe department. A large four-letter sign caught my eye: SALE. On the counter sat a fine pair of handmade Cole Haan shoes. They were beautiful. I put them on. I'm talking happy feet! Comfortable shoes. It was like wearing socks. I took off the left shoe and turned it over to see the price tag. It said $425. Where I live, $425 is what we call a house payment. I took off the shoes, blew inside them to make sure I hadn't left any sweat in there, placed them on the counter, and put my shoes back on.

The young salesperson working in that shoe department called to me. "Tell me those shoes are your size."

"Those shoes are my size," I said.

"You are a lucky man," he said.

I'm not $425 worth of lucky, I thought to myself.

He said, "That is the best-selling shoe we've had this year. I've sold more of those shoes than I have of any other style. As a matter of fact, I've sold more of those shoes than most of our other styles of shoes put together. And that, sir, is the last pair. That shoe has been marked down to $69.95."

Now, $69.95 fit my price range. So I placed them back on my feet again, giving them another test-drive. Trying on shoes at Neiman Marcus is very different from trying on shoes in other department stores I've been in. In many stores you get only one shoe to try on, and you walk around kind of hobbling because one leg is longer than the other. As I walked around with those two beautiful shoes on my feet, I looked at the young salesperson and said, "Would it be OK if I wore them out of the store?"

That probably was a lapse in judgment on my part. He didn't say anything, but I could sense that he thought that I probably shopped at Wal-Mart. But he didn't miss a beat. "Of course you can wear those shoes out! Why don't you allow me to ship your other shoes home for you?"

"You'd do that?"

"Certainly! I'd love to."

Maybe my sense of humor is a little different, but I was thinking that every postal clerk between Washington, D.C., and Harriman, Tennessee, would smell that box and say, "You know, I think something has died in there!"

Seven weeks later we went back to serve the same client. Same short notice, same four-hour layover. Same secretary saying, "Let's go shopping."

"No," I said. "Let's go to Neiman's."

I walked through the men's shoe department, hoping that I would meet my young friend and that there would be some more shoes on sale. Alas! There was no sale. As I headed for the exit I heard, "Dr. Henry, I see you are wearing your shoes!"

I turned around, and there stood my young salesperson. "I love these shoes!" I said. "I love my shoes so much that if my wife would let me, I'd sleep in them."

"Have you had an opportunity to have them polished yet?" he asked.

"You know what? I did. I flew into Dulles this morning, and I had them polished." (When I talk about something, I tend to look at it.) I looked down at my shoes and said, "You know, what I really like about these shoes is the way the leather is woven together, the way the handmade weaving of the shoe makes it unique. I noticed that when they were polished this morning the leather didn't take polish quite the same over here on the side of the left shoe. That's how you can tell they are handmade."

And I looked up. You know how silly you feel when you've been talking to your shoes for about 30 seconds and you look up and there's no one there? Well, there was one woman with a small child, whom she quickly pulled to one side and said, "Now, let's go over here, and let the nice man talk to his shoes."

Then my young sales friend came out from behind the curtain. I didn't have my glasses on, but I could see the price on the box he was holding—almost $600. "There's a defect in the leather of those shoes that you have on. That's why it's not taking polish the way it should. I insist that we exchange them."

I started doing the math and decided immediately that I liked the shoes I had on. I thought he wanted me to exchange and pay the difference. That's when I got a shock.

"Dr. Henry, I really must insist that we exchange shoes evenly."

There are two things that I want to call to your attention. This young man remembered my name. We had had only one interaction, and that had been seven weeks before. You might be thinking that my Southern accent gave him a clue. Or possibly that it was because I wore my shoes out of the store that day I bought them and that he had had to ship my other shoes home.

It could have been a lot of things, but it impressed me when he called me by name. It also impressed me when he wanted to exchange shoes evenly. That's just not something that's done—a sale shoe for a full-priced shoe.

That's when he did it. That's when this young salesperson reminded me of what I already knew, because I had heard it before. My sales manager at Miller's department store had told me the same philosophy years before. I hadn't heard it then, but I heard it this time, and it has changed the way I look at serving others.

"Dr. Henry, this is Neiman Marcus," he said. "At Neiman Marcus we don't just sell products—we give service. We don't want you just to buy things here; we want you to do business with us. Those shoes you have on are defective, and I insist that we exchange and that we exchange evenly. Your business is that important to me." Then he said it: "Dr. Henry, at Neiman Marcus the customer is always served."

He didn't say, "The customer is always right"; he said, "The customer is always served."

Many of us are in business and serve clients. The difference is that in this day and age, when someone is dissatisfied with the customer service they receive, they don't complain and whine about that service. They merely take their business elsewhere. So our level of commitment to service needs to be higher. That's what Solomon was talking about in Proverbs. Unless we are willing to go that extra mile in providing service, we should not expect someone to go that extra mile to be served by us.

I was meeting with some young sales managers at Marriott. One young man named Mark asked me, "Dr. Henry, how do we set ourselves apart in serving our clients?"

"We think differently," I told him. "We look at what everybody else does; then we do something that goes a little further down that path. We are driven to serve, and we are driven by our commitment to be different."

He asked me to explain, and I took the challenge. "Tell me, what do you do on a day-to-day basis?"

"Well, I talk to customers. I talk to clients who are interested in using our hotel."

"Would you like to see your closure rate higher?"

"Of course."

"That closure rate is directly connected to how committed you are to serving them, how committed you are to showing them that you are different. In our society we become a bit homogenized. What many of us see when we come to a hotel is the difference in the brand name—Marriott or Hilton, Hyatt or Crowne Plaza. That's all we see, because what's on the inside tends to be approximately the same.

"What we have to do is change that. So let's play a game. Let's pretend that I'm a customer who comes into your hotel. Let's say I have 500 people who want to go to a conference here. We're going to stay three days and are going to use meeting rooms. You are going to feed us. You know all the things you're going to have to do. It's not my business, so I don't know it as well as you do. So tell me, after we have a conversation, after we talk about some of my needs and I leave, you are going to follow up. Is that correct?"

"Well, yes, Dr. Henry, that's exactly correct."

"What are you going to do?"

"Well, I'm going to send a card and a personalized letter telling you how much we would like to have you come and do your business with us."

"Mark, what do you think the people down at the Hyatt are going to do?"

He smiled. "The same thing."

"How about at the Hilton? the Crowne Plaza? the Omni?"

"They're all going to do the same thing, Dr. Henry."

"Yeah, they are. So why would you do the same thing? Does that show commitment?"

"No, sir," he said.

"Let's try attacking this in a different way."

He settled back to listen.

I said, "Instead of sending a packet, which you've sent out a million times before, how about using your brain? Go down to the gift shop and purchase a 24-exposure disposable camera. Go out to the conference area where there is a conference going on that is the same size as the conference you are trying to sell. Take pictures of people in meeting rooms, people in break areas, people enjoying the food, pictures of the different decorations that you've done for that conference's theme. Take pictures of people using the phones and pictures showing how convenient those phones and the bathrooms are to the conference rooms that they will be using.

"Save the last photograph for one special shot. Since you are interested in getting this information to your client in a timely manner, and since you also want your potential client to know that you did this for them this morning after they left, wrap a $20 bill around that camera. Send it with the usual thank-you letter and all the information you include in your packet. Drop in a blank cassette tape and put this note on the outside:

" 'Please do not listen to this cassette until you have developed the film. I apologize for sending the camera undeveloped, but I wanted you to know that I took these pictures this morning. In my desire to serve you quickly, I'm asking that you have the film developed.' "

I continued: "Now, Mark, what's the one thing you want this customer to do?"

"To call me back," he replied.

"Let's go to that customer's office in our imagination and watch as they open the packet and dump out the contents. They're surprised to see a disposable camera with a $20 bill wrapped around it. They read your note and see the cassette tape with the message that instructs them not to listen to it until they develop the film. What does human nature tell you they're going to do with that cassette?"

"They're going to listen to it."

"And when they listen to it, they're going to hear nothing but white sound—absolutely nothing! They're going to assume one of two things: either the cassette tape is broken, or the tape you sent is defective. They will then call you, and that's your opportunity to serve them. That's your opportunity to show them your level of commitment."

Mark had a confused look on his face, so I said, "That's when you tell them, 'I wish you had waited until you had developed the film. Then you would have understood the tape. You see, the last picture on that roll is me, standing in a meeting room next to the meeting room where 500 of our customers were having a seminar. The reason you hear nothing but white sound on the tape is that we are interested in keeping your room quiet for your meeting, regardless of who's next door. You see, I want to serve you, and I want you to know how interested we are in making your meeting a successful one."

These young sales managers could hardly wait to leave the room! They wanted to apply the information that I had given them. But I'm not that smart. I try to imagine myself in the role of the customer, because I have been there many times. I like that feeling of being able to look at a problem, not from my perspective, but the perspective of others. If we can do that, we can become the prize. We can get out of the box.

The same process that I took the young hotel sales managers through, I had the opportunity to do for employees of an insurance company that sold corporate insurance. I asked them to explain to me why they thought they weren't closing on a lot of their potential commercial clients. They went through their procedures, describing for me exactly what they did. I stopped looking at it as a salesperson would and started looking at it as a client would.

"So let's stop a moment and recap," I said. "You come into an office and ask to look at their insurance policies. Let's assume it's on worker's compensation. Then you go back to the office and do the research. You check the many companies you represent. You find them a good deal with better coverage, because you have found holes in some of the things that they need to be covered for. You do your homework very well. You go back with an insurance policy that's not only better but less expensive. You lay that insurance policy and prospective contract on the client's desk. Is that close so far?"

The insurance personnel nodded.

"OK, what do you think that customer is going to do when you leave? They're going to pick up the phone and call the insurance agent they've been dealing with for the past 10 years. They're going to tell that agent that someone just called on them and gave them a better policy with better coverage for less money. Their insurance agent is going to say, 'Well, I can match that.' All your homework, all your research, is going to be for nothing.

"Because you didn't go the extra step, all you have done, essentially, is make the sale for someone else. You didn't show the client that you were committed to serving them..

"Try this. After you do the research and get your insurance policy with a better deal and better coverage ready, go back to that office and sit down. Ask some questions:

" 'Does the representative of the insurance company you are using now come by every quarter? Does that representative take a look at your insurance and try to show you how to get the best deal with the best coverage? Or do they call on you only when it's time to renew? Probably the latter. This insurance agent with whom you are dealing now, what level of trust do you have in them? Do you include them in your circle of friends?

"'I want to be in that circle. My commitment to you is that I want you to prosper, because I know if you prosper, I'll prosper. You see, I know what you are going to do when I give you this insurance contract. You are going to call this person who has not been serving you, and, of course, they are probably going to match my price and my coverage. So you see, in reality, the difference between the business side of what we do and what your current agent does is that *I'm* different. I believe that the customer is always served.'"

What we are talking about here isn't rocket science. It's using common sense. But common sense isn't very common, and it isn't very intelligent. Common sense is simply the information you use in making decisions. It's about taking that information and flipping it around the other way. Why do you buy? Well, if you know why someone buys something, if you know why you buy something, that same philosophy will also help you, because what you want is to be served. You want to be treated right.

I get to stay in some of the nicest hotels in the country, and after a while that spoils you. I was in Jasper, Indiana, doing a program for Jasper Engines and Transmissions. I was given a choice of a couple of hotels to stay in. They weren't what you'd call full-service hotels, which I like because usually you can get a meal and don't have to do a lot of driving. Since I like to prepare for a presentation, I like a little time to sit and reflect, as opposed to driving around trying to find a place to eat.

Because this particular town wasn't a booming metropolis with lots of big-name hotels, I stayed at a Sleep Inn. This was my first experience at a Sleep Inn, and I was delightfully surprised. A cordial young man graciously greeted me when I walked in. I have been greeted no better at any fine five-star hotel. I asked him if I might have a room that would be close to the front—quiet, away from the ice machine. He accommodated me.

Before I left the lobby he said, "Dr. Henry, you know we have a complimentary breakfast in the morning. Simply fill out what you would like to eat and the time you would like to eat it, and we will deliver it to your door." You can have that done in a full-service hotel, but it's not included in the price of a night's stay, which at the Sleep Inn was very reasonable.

The first thing I noticed when I got to my room was that there was no tub. Excellent! I don't like baths. I'm a shower kind of guy. The shower in the Sleep Inn was huge. I could literally stand in the middle of the shower, extend my arms out by my sides, and turn without touching the wall. For those of you who stay in a lot of hotels, you know that's cool, because, number one, the shower curtain usually has a chemical in it that causes the shower curtain to be attracted to the body. I hate that.

Number two, I hate baths because as a young boy I took baths in a No. 10 washtub (we didn't have indoor plumbing). A No. 10 washtub is just big enough to get a kid in. As I sat there in that tub in the kitchen one time, my grandfather went by. Looking me right in the eye, he said, "Boy, don't ever take a bath, because you are washing your face in the same water you are sitting in." I've never forgotten his good advice.

Just down the street was a nice little restaurant, where I had a good meal. When I came back to the hotel I stopped by my young friend at the counter and asked, "Where's your drink machine?"

"Dr. Henry, it's right down the hall from your room, about seven or eight doors down on the left. Can I get something for you?"

"No, no; I just wanted a Sprite to drink while I was doing a little reading this evening. I'll see you in the morning."

"I hope you sleep well, sir," he said.

I went back to the drink machine. I hate drink machines that take dollar bills, because I always feel a little geeky standing there feeding it in, only to have it pushed back out. That's when I looked at the drink machine and saw that every light on the machine was on—it was out of drinks. I went back to the front desk and asked if there was a convenience store nearby.

"Yes, there is. What is it you need?"

"Well, your drink machine is out of drinks, and—"

"Oh, I'm so sorry. One of our employees didn't come in today, and they probably didn't fill the machine up. I apologize."

"No, no, no," I said. "This sort of stuff happens. I'll just go slip on my shoes and go down to the little convenience store and get myself a soda."

I had barely gotten back to my room and slipped on one of my shoes when there was a knock at the door. There stood my young friend with two Sprites in an ice bucket. "Dr. Henry, I hate that you have to put your shoes on to go get a drink. I just went back to the stockroom and put two Sprites in this ice. I apologize for the inconvenience. I hope this meets your needs."

Sleep Inn . . . They have Serta mattresses on their beds, and I slept like a dream. The next morning my breakfast was delivered to my door. And I had valet service bringing me soda. All for $39.95, plus tax. Pretty amazing. I still like full-service hotels, and I do a lot of business with many of them. But if I'm driving down the road and need a place to stay, I go to a Sleep Inn. Why? Because I was served. Because they showed me—no, they *zinged* me—with an altogether new level of service.

And I was impressed.

12

Zing Your Ability to Lead and Follow

"It wasn't me!" Getting past excuses that keep us from excelling.

He who leads the upright along an evil path will fall into his own trap.—PROVERBS 28:10.

The difference between success and failure isn't always ability. Sometimes it's a little thing like attitude, the way we look at the world around us. When they meet me, most people believe I have a perfect life. That could be true. It's perfect in my eyes. I have a wonderful wife who loves me, and whom I love very much. I have two wonderful daughters. I have a roof over my head and food in my stomach. I am in good health. Why shouldn't I have the perfect life?

Don't get me wrong. I have day-to-day problems. We all do. What makes a life perfect isn't living—it's expectation.

Earlier in the book we talked about expecting the best. In this chapter we're going to get past the things that slow us up and keep us from excelling. We're going to move on to a more positive and more power-packed way of living. When people see me on stage they often come up to me afterward and tell me how blessed I am. I don't argue with them. I agree with them. But my life isn't always perfect. There are those times when things go wrong, and, believe me, when they go wrong they go very wrong.

I was once doing a program that started out like any other

program. The meeting planner had asked me to do an evening keynote address, something I do often and love to do. I asked what the rest of the day's activities were going to look like in an effort to help my client achieve her goal. She said that the CEO of the company was going to speak for a couple of hours, followed by a well-known speaker, who was going to do a program. That evening I would do the keynote.

I called the speaker because I wanted to know what topics he was going to cover. He gave me the cold shoulder. I don't know why. I assume it was because he was guarding his material closely. I explained that my only interest in learning about his program was to help our client. He wasn't belligerent, just rather obnoxious. After about 15 minutes of jockeying for position, he agreed that he'd give me a brief outline of his presentation.

I arrived on site and sat down in the meeting with Bill Karlson, a good friend from Nashville, Tennessee. Bill and I took seats to the left of the lectern where we would be out of the way but could observe, and I could take notes to be more prepared for that evening's presentation.

What happened next was a little scary. The CEO got up in front of almost 500 managers with a stack of paper that turned out to be complaint letters. Having each manager stand up, he would read the letter. That was his entire presentation. He ran out of time before he ran out of letters. I don't know what the purpose of the exercise was. I thought perhaps the speaker who was to precede me would straighten it out. But he pretty much talked along the same lines that the CEO had. He complained about the hotel in which we were staying—the hot water wasn't working in his room. He complained about the service and, overall, about the property.

At 5:00 these people left the room. By that time they no doubt knew exactly how many ceiling tiles were in that meeting facility. Between 5:00 and 6:30 the attendees had free time. At 7:00 we moved into the meeting room again, where we were fed from 8:00 to 9:00. Then I was to conclude the meeting.

How would you like to have been in my shoes? My friend, Bill Karlson, told me there was no way in the world he would get up there. I am an inspirational humorist, not a motivational speaker. These people didn't need motivation, however; they needed hope. The way the riser was positioned, I was standing in front of the head table. I informed the CEO and those in leadership that unless they liked looking at the back of my head they might want to find a seat in the audience. They chose not to do that, separating themselves from the people they were leading.

Two minutes before my presentation, the CEO's wife, who was positioned directly behind me, informed me that she was narcoleptic and at any moment could fall asleep during my presentation.

It was not a good day. But as I told you, a good day has nothing to do with the situations in which you find yourself. A good day is what you make it, and I decided to make it a good day. My 45- to 50-minute presentation turned into 90 minutes. Oh, I knew what time it was. But I decided in that presentation that I would use the negatives we had heard that day so that the attendees would leave in a positive light.

To say it went very well would be an understatement. They enjoyed the presentation so much that by the time I left, my right arm was sore from being shaken. I would say that fewer than 5 percent of them did not come up and talk to me, and I think the reason they didn't come was that they were in the lobby purchasing tapes and videos of other presentations.

Why was what I did so successful? They were hungry. They were hungry for an attitude of can-do. They were hungry for someone to tell them that it's easy to get past excuses. What's hard is getting on with life.

In this chapter we're going to review option thinking and how to separate *can't* from *won't*. We're also going to look at ways to deal with people when they are eager to say that something can't be accomplished. I believe in the power of one. I believe that one person can—and will—change the world. Many people will doubt this, and that's OK. But that doesn't change the fact that one person can make a difference. The example I just gave you described a challenging day. On occasion I do programs that I would call perfect. Let me tell you about a perfect program.

A client wanted me to come to Florida for four days. This was in January. I live in the South but not the Deep South, so we have cold weather. Being in Florida in January was good news. I was going to arrive at this program about 4:30 p.m. Again, good news. I don't like getting to a strange town when it's dark. I don't do very well in the dark. (If you are 45 years old or older, you will understand that.)

I learned that during three of the four days that I was doing presentations we were going to be playing golf. Not once or twice—three times! I love to play golf. So here I was, caught in the middle of what I would call a perfect presentation.

I was going to be able to take clothes. Clothes are an interesting option for me. I don't check luggage, so if I'm on the road for four, five, or six days, I have to be very frugal in the way I pack my luggage. I have to be thinking about every program, about every item of clothing, all the way down to underwear and socks. For this program I would be in the same town for four days. I could pack clothes. I could check luggage. I could take shoes, shirts, and suits to speak in; clothes to play golf in; and clothes to relax and have dinner in.

This could have been the perfect program had it not been for the airline, which didn't see my perfect program as perfect. Instead of arriving at 4:30, I got there at 6:30. I arrived at this absolutely gorgeous resort with just a glimmer of daylight left. It turned out to be what I refer to as a la-di-da resort. As I pulled up to the front gate you would have thought I was trying to get into the Pentagon. I had to show my license, they wrote down the tag of my rental car, and I had to give my sponsor's name.

Once all these things were checked, I was told to proceed to the check-in office of the resort. I walked into the registration building and said, "Hello, my name is Dale Henry. I believe I have a reservation."

Have you ever had someone who looks at you after you finish

speaking to them, and then turns their head to the side like a beagle pup? You know there was something you said that was interesting. In this case the young man behind the counter said, "Where are you from?"

"I live in Harriman, Tennessee."

"You're not going to believe this, but I am from Crossville."

If you're from the South, and you're in a strange city and meet someone who lives less than 20 minutes away from you, you are going to talk. And we did. We talked for about an hour. In the meantime it got dark. Not just dark—pitch-black dark. No moon, no stars, no nothing. He gave me a key, looked over to his right, and ripped a map off the wall. That was not good news. As much as we men would like to tell you that we are very good at instructions and directions, we are not. He told me I would turn beside the registration office and drive a quarter of a mile. I would go over a bridge and turn left. I would go about three quarters of a mile and come to two bridges. I would drive until I came to a palm tree and turn left again. I would go to Building B, third floor, condominium 26.

I went out and sat in my car. The young man had outlined my journey on the map in yellow. You can't see yellow in a dark car. If you're more than 45 and you've ever been lost, you know the posture I was getting ready to assume: I grabbed the top of the steering wheel and hoisted my body so that my chin was slightly in front of the top of the steering wheel. I squinted, somewhat like a turtle, and turned on the dome light so that I could read the directions better. Unfortunately, turning on the light turned the windshield into a mirror, which was impossible to see through.

That's when I thought, *Hey, I'm a man. I can follow directions.* This would be the first of several inaccurate thoughts that night. Getting to the hotel late, not knowing where I was going, and having to follow directions in the dark, were just a few of the things that were trying to spoil my perfect program. And, of course, my young friend had sent me on my way with that most fearful of phrases: "You can't miss it."

In my desperation to find my room by memory, I started down the road. I came to the bridge. "Right, I believe he said. Yes, right." I turned right and immediately got hopelessly lost. One of life's truisms is that when you get lost, the first person you come to will be one who does not like to give directions. This person, with some reluctance, told me how to get where I was going and, of course, told me that I turned the wrong way but not to worry: "You can't miss it."

Driving back, I found the two bridges. That's when it occurred to me that I was in southern Florida, and in southern Florida there are about a gazillion palm trees. Why hadn't he mentioned that it was a *neon* palm tree? I turned left, found Building B, and started to unload my luggage. (You do remember the luggage, right? I had lots of luggage.)

The wonderful thing about la-di-da properties is that normally you have people who will help you check into your room. This resort was so la-di-da that the folks checking in there brought their own people. I didn't have people. I had me. Like an old pack mule, I loaded up, and I walked (yes, I said walked) up the three flights of stairs. This resort, although very la-di-da, was older, and elevators were not an option.

I made it to the third floor and found my condominium. I slid in my key and wiggled and jiggled it. I slid it in and out. It didn't work. My dad had always told me, "Son, when a key does not work in a lock, just spit on it." Don't ask me why. I just did it, then stuck the key back in. I wiggled it and I jiggled it. I slid it in and out. Of course, it didn't work. It wasn't the right key.

I sighed, threw my luggage over my shoulder and under my arms and went back down to my car. I loaded up and headed back to the resort office and, of course, got lost.

"How do you like your condo?" my young friend from Crossville greeted me.

I eyed him carefully. "You know, the property is beautiful, but I haven't seen my condo yet." I told him that the key he had given me didn't work.

A disembodied voice from somewhere behind the counter demanded, "Well, did you wiggle it? Did you jiggle it? Did you slide it in and out?"

I answered in the affirmative.

Maintenance man Leon stepped up to the front desk, looked at the key, eyeballing its notches and grooves. "I believe that's the right key," he declared. "Are you sure you know how to use it?"

Still in perfect control, I said, "Yes, I'm pretty sure I know how to use a key. I've seen many of them. I have a Ph.D. Yup, I know how to use a key."

He said, "Let's just run you down there and get you in your room."

I was happy. First, because we were making positive progress. Second, because I wouldn't have to worry about getting lost. I could follow him to the room. He jumped into his truck. We drove a quarter of a mile, passed over the bridge, turned left, went three quarters of a mile over both bridges, came to the neon palm tree, hung a left, and went to the Building B parking lot.

In my brain I was thinking, *H'mmm. Now I've got somebody to help with my luggage.* I shouldn't have had that thought. Somehow it passed through my brain, through my car, and through the atmosphere between our cars, and into his car. When he stepped out of his truck, he grabbed his back and cried, "Ooh! My back is killing me!"

Loading my luggage on every available body surface, I slowly followed Leon up the steps to condominium 26, where he stuck in the key. Yes, he wiggled and he jiggled it, and he slid it in and out. But it did not work. He took his flashlight from his tool belt and shone it on the key. Then he looked at me and said, "Here's your problem. Look at this. That lock somehow has gotten wet."

All I could think to say was "I can't imagine how that could have happened."

He sprayed it with WD-40 and put the key back in the lock and did the wiggle-jiggle thing again. I can only tell you that at this point in history he could wiggle and jiggle his brains out, but that key wasn't going to work, because it wasn't the right key. If you've ever met a maintenance man, you know that maintenance men carry keys. As a matter of fact, they carry many keys—hundreds of keys. Not Leon. He had *a* key, the key that I gave him.

He said, "I'm going to run down there and get you another key. You wait right here."

I'm not sure how well traveled you are, but the one place you do not want to be on this planet is in south Florida at night beneath a lightbulb, not without a blood transfusion available, anyway. Twenty-five minutes went by. Thirty-five, 45, 55 minutes. An hour passed by. Looking off into the darkness, I could only think, *He's dead. He has driven off into the swamp. An alligator ate him, and I'm the only one who knows I'm here.*

So I carried my things back to my car and drove to the resort. (Successfully, I might add. I'd been down that road before.) I walked into the office. My young friend from Crossville was still there. Once again he inquired about my accommodations.

"I haven't seen my condominium yet," I said.

From behind the counter came the now-familiar disembodied voice. "Uh-oh. I forgot you. Let's run you down there, though, and get you in your room."

I don't need to remind you of the road so often traveled. You could probably find your way on your own. I loaded my stuff onto my back. Back up the three flights we went up, step by slow step. Once again we stood in front of condominium 26, and he slid in the key, and we heard the incomparable sound a correct key makes as it turns the tumblers. The door was opened.

That's when he said, "Uh-oh. There's no furniture in this room."

There wasn't any carpet, either. There was a commode leaning up against the wall, but it didn't work.

"You know," he said, "I'll bet this is one of those rooms they are remodeling."

You think?

"Let's go down to the office and get you another room," he suggested.

If you've been taking any kind of notice as to how many trips to that office I'd taken, and if you have been keeping track of time, you'll know that it was then almost midnight. I had been trying to get into a room for four hours.

I'm going to stop the story for a couple of reasons. You are probably going to guess that by then I was mad. I wasn't. I don't get mad. Mad doesn't accomplish anything other than to make your blood pressure rise. In reality I had no reason to be upset—I wasn't hurt. Oh, I was inconvenienced, but we all get inconvenienced. I didn't want to be inconvenienced, but even more, I didn't want to become angry. I'll have to admit, though, that the coating on my happy pill was getting thin. If at this point I pulled out a customer satisfaction rating card on this resort, 10 being "This is the best service I have ever received in my entire life" and 0 being "Why is this happening to me?" where do you think we'd be on the rating scale? I'll let you decide.

My young friend from Crossville was not in the office. His shift was over. In his place stood the night manager of the property. His face was as red as a pickled beet, as we say in the South. Not from anger—from embarrassment.

"Dr. Henry, of all the people whose rooms we could mess up on, it had to be the speaker's room. You talk about this kind of stuff, don't you?" He had no way of knowing that I don't talk about negative stories (unless there's a positive ending).

"Yes, I do on occasion," I said.

"Hand me your car keys," he said.

I'm thinking, *Great. No room, and now no car. I'm going to have to curl up on the couch with Leon.*

The manager went outside and unloaded my luggage, that big trunkful of luggage that I had brought from home. He put it on the curb. He looked for anything I might have left inside the car. There was nothing. I don't put anything on the seat but the contract the rental car company gives me. He got into my car and drove it around to the back of the building. I would never see that car again.

When he came back he was driving a white limousine. He opened the trunk and put my things inside. He opened the back door and motioned for me to come outside. I got in and sat down. Now, if you are more than 45 years old, you know that at night—a dark night with no stars and no moon—you can't see diddly. You also know that from the back of a limousine you can see even less. I did, however, recognize that we weren't going down that old familiar path.

We drove for a moment, then slipped off on one of those sandy, seashell-type roads that make a popping and crackling sound under the tires of the car. We were on that road for 20 minutes, then came to a bridge. Oh, that lovely sound as the tires roll over the boards! Then the sound of seashells and sand again, popping and crackling beneath the wheels of the limousine.

Then we stopped. My driver got out of the car and came around and opened the door. I immediately knew I wasn't at Building B, condominium 26. I was on an island, a rather small island. In the center of this island was a beautiful villa.

"Dr. Henry, I don't know how this happened, but it did. Apologizing would probably be fruitless at this point."

He could see that I wasn't upset, but he could also see that, being a human being, I had been somewhat put off.

"I guess you noticed I pulled your car around to the back of the building. You won't be needing it during the next three and a half days here at our resort. We will send our limo driver, Rich, and he is going to take care of you. This villa that you are standing in front of is our owner's villa. He's in Europe for the next two months. I'm sure he won't mind your being here, because we let our most honored guests stay here.

"There are some unusual features about it, though, that I almost feel obligated to tell you about. There's no phone. There's no television. There are no clocks or radios. You are probably wondering why a beautiful villa like this would have none of those modern conveniences in it. Our owner says that without these things time seems to stop. In paradise you want that to happen. Because there is no way of us contacting you or you contacting us, I will need to know your schedule. What time would you like to get up in the morning?"

"Oh, 6:30 would be good. I am speaking at 9:00. I would like to get in a run."

"Well, Dr. Henry," he said, "unless you like just running around and around, since this is an island, I recommend that Rich come down and pick you up. He'll wake you up at 6:30 and wait for you to get ready. He'll take you to our running track, which runs parallel to our golf course. This will give you an opportunity to get the lay of the course. Since I noticed you have your clubs in here, I assume you are playing golf while you are staying with us."

"Yes. I am playing golf for the next three days."

"Wonderful. I'll just take your clubs up to the clubhouse and let them clean them up for you." He put my clubs back into the limo.

As we walked toward the villa with my luggage he said, "After Rich comes down and gets you to take you to the running track, he will wait for you. He will then drive you back to the villa. On the way back he'll ask you what you would like for breakfast. We'll send someone down from our catering staff to fix your breakfast in your villa. After breakfast Rich will take you to your meeting, pick you up, bring you back, let you change your clothes, and take you to the golf course. Rich will be your transportation, as well as your wake-up call and your contact, here at the resort."

We walked through the front door. The villa was absolutely gorgeous.

"I envy you," he said. "Oh, not because you will be staying in this beautiful facility, but because this villa has seven bedrooms. I recommend that you pick out your favorite three and spend one night in each one of those rooms, not because they have beautiful views, but because they are all very different."

He said good night and left. On my belt was a cell phone. I looked down and saw a green flashing light, which meant my service was working. I called my wife because I know Debra doesn't sleep well until I call her. Her first words were "You must have had an eventful day."

"Oh, it wasn't bad," I said.

"If you are calling this late, it must have been something," she said. I said, "How are you?"

"Good."

"Did the girls have a good day?"

"Yes."

"Why don't you go to bed, honey, and I'll talk to you tomorrow."

"Well, tell me, at least, were your expectations met? You were so excited about your trip."

"Oh, honey, I wish you were here. Life is good in Florida."

Let's take out the customer satisfaction rating card again, 10 being "the best service I have ever received," and 0 being "I can't believe this is happening to me." Any change? Any adjustments? I thought so.

What was the difference? Did the property undergo a major overhaul while I was there? No more than normal.

Maybe the staff changed, and they hired a bunch of new people and had a good training program going on.

No. Same personnel, same people working there.

New management, I'll bet.

No. Same group, nothing changed.

What did change was one person. The power of one. One individual taking responsibility in a positive way and moving forward. That's the power of the story.

It wasn't the beautiful room or the villa. It wasn't Rich and how wonderfully he took care of me, which he did. It wasn't the beautiful golf course or the wonderful running track or the gorgeous surroundings.

They added to my enjoyment during my time there, and I want you to know that it was one of the most perfect programs I ever did. Not only was the quality of the program good, but wow, what a resort!

The power of one. This story sticks in my head because on occasion I run into people who say, "Well, you know, one person can't change things."

Oh, my friend! One person can change it *all*. If, like me, you believe in Christ, you know that one person can make all the difference in the world. He can take chaos and turn it into a miracle. He can take a wasted life and turn it into a glorious one that's worth living.

The power of one. Pretty strong! This isn't the only time I have seen the power of one.

I was getting ready to give a presentation at a small Marriott. Again I saw the power of one, that amazing ability one person has to turn an experience that could have been negative into one that was positive. On this trip I had decided to wear my jogging clothes. I was going to run when I got to the resort, then go to bed, get up the next morning, do this program, and drive home.

I got there, and I ran. I went to bed and got up the next morning. I had an early program and had plenty of time to get ready. I put on my clothes and sat down to watch a show on television that I sometimes watch. I got up, opened my bag, and, to my horror, discovered that I had packed one brown shoe and one black shoe. There was no similarity between them at all—one was a slip-on, and the other one tied.

This wasn't good. I had 40 minutes until I was on, so I called the front desk. I did this because of that little sign that's in the bathroom of most hotels: "If you have forgotten anything, give us a call at the front desk." I wasn't anticipating that the front desk had shoes, but they might be able to tell me where to go to get them quickly. A young male voice answered my ring.

"Is there any place close by where I might be able to get some shoes?"

"Yes, sir," he said. "There's a small mall nearby."

"It's not open now, though, is it?"

"No, not for another hour."

"How about a Wal-Mart? Anything?"

"Well, there is one, but it's about 30 minutes away. Sir, what can I help you with? How can I serve you?"

"I need a pair of shoes," I told him. "I packed a brown one and a black one, and I'm getting ready to do a presentation. I'm sunk, because if you know anything, you know that people notice what kind of shoes the speaker has on, especially since I'll be standing up there where they can see my shoes almost at eye level."

Then he said the strangest thing. "What size shoes do you wear?"

"I wear a size eight."

"Eight D be OK?" he asked.

"Eight D is perfect."

I went downstairs, and on the counter of that registration desk was a pair of black Loafers. I threw them on the ground, slipped my feet inside, and, thanking him profusely, ran off to my meeting.

Two hours later I came back. I put the shoes back on the desk and said to the young man, "You know, I love staying at Marriott, and I find their service to be exemplary, no matter where I am in the country. But I have to tell you, I am astonished that you folks keep shoes."

"Oh, we don't keep shoes, Dr. Henry." He held up his sock foot and said, "They are *my* shoes."

The power of one. A person's ability to set themselves apart.

I have one more story I would like to share with you. I don't use Enterprise rental cars very often. Sometimes their airport locations are a bit difficult to get to. On this occasion I decided I would rent from them. The young woman who picked me up from the airport in the van was beyond courteous—she was outstandingly courteous.

When we got to the rental office, she got out and helped me with my luggage. She walked me into the rental office and introduced me to Chuck.

"Mr. Henry," she said, "this is Chuck. He will be helping you with your rental car."

Chuck then said, "Mr. Henry, what kind of rental car would you like?"

"Well, I'm just going about an hour up the road. I'd like something with cruise control on it."

"OK. Do you have a preference for color or make or model?"

"Well, not really."

"How about a Jeep Cherokee?"

"You know, I have a Jeep Cherokee. That would make me feel comfortable."

"We don't have any smaller cars, so the reason I asked you was that I'm going to give you a Jeep Cherokee for the price of a compact car."

"Thank you," I said.

Usually at this point in the renting of a car I am signing the contract, and they're handing me the keys and telling me the parking lot number. I walk out, find the car, jump in it, and go on my way.

"So you have good directions where you are going?" he asked.

"Yes, I do. I have a MapBlast! in my briefcase."

"Well, where are you going, anyway, Mr. Henry? Sometimes those MapBlasts! maps are good; sometimes they're not. I may know a better way."

I told him where I was going, and he said, "You know, this is going to take you on a major highway. If you like seeing scenery and you're not in a big hurry, let me recommend a road that won't get you there any quicker, but it sure will be a lot more enjoyable."

Not only did he give me a map, but he drew it by hand, indicating the lefts and rights, and noting what to watch for before I made those turns.

He then walked me to the car. When I sat down in the car, he asked me if I was comfortable with all the options, and stood there while I started it.

He said, "Now, here's my card. If there's anything I can do, or if you have any problems at all, call me. There's a 24-hour number on there that will get me."

The power of one. Did I rent from Enterprise again? Of course! Have I found the same type of friendly service? Overall, yes. One person caused me to change. I will tell you that when I am back in that city, I always go to that Enterprise. I always ask for Chuck.

The power of one. Most people want to know why it works so effectively. Why can one person can make such a difference? It might be that most of us don't know much about the people we work with on a daily basis. We certainly don't know about those we work with on a temporary one. One of the strongest mechanisms that drives leadership, that drives this ability to get past excuses and get on to excelling, is that we become the known.

Not too long ago I was on the radio show of a good friend. Remember Bill Karlson from earlier in this chapter? (Bill has written a wonderful book entitled *Get Top $$$ in a Job You Love!*) As his guest on that show, I talked with him about many issues.

One day as we were talking he said, "Dale, of all the things that you talk about, of all the issues you cover as you travel around the country, which one seems to be the most powerful?"

I said, "I have to answer that by telling you that it's the power of one—it's one person's ability to change the world. But hidden inside that property of becoming and understanding the power of one is becoming the known."

He seemed to be intrigued.

I said, "Bill, I'd love to talk about becoming the known; unfortunately, we don't have time to cover that topic in the last five minutes of your show. Maybe I could come back on another show, and we could talk about it then."

When we were off the air, he said, "Tell me more about becoming the known."

"I've been away from my family for about four days, Bill. They were kind enough to drive with me to Nashville so I could be on your radio show. They're outside now, and they are starving to death. Listen, both you and I are going to Bermuda in a week. Why don't we meet in Atlanta? We can sit together on the plane, and we can talk about this issue all the way there. That way we'll be more prepared to discuss it intelligently on the next radio show."

Now, Bill, being a lot like me, didn't think about seating on that plane. Because of the many air miles I have, I was sitting in first class. Bill was in coach. We couldn't have a good conversation that way, but we decided when we got to the gate that we would get our seats together. That's when we heard that announcement in Atlanta: "Ladies and gentlemen, we are in an oversold situation. If you can make your travel plans a little bit later in the day, we will be glad to give you a free ticket."

We looked at each other and had the same thought: *We ain't sitting together!*

Bill looked at me and said, "Dale, you told me that becoming the known was the most powerful thing to help you get from point A to point B in your quest for success."

"That's right. I really, honestly believe it is."

"Show me."

I like challenges. "OK, Bill, what do you want?"

"I want us to sit together."

"OK, sit together we will."

He grinned. "I've got to see this."

We got in line to get our boarding passes. I noticed that the young woman who was checking us in was wearing a red jacket. On Delta Airlines a red jacket indicates that the person is a supervisor. I watched her for a few minutes, then informed Bill that I was ready to get in line.

Making our way to the front of that line, I walked up to the counter. The tag on the red jacket said her name was Ann.

"Yes, sir, how may I help you?"

"Hi, Ann. My name is Dale Henry."

"Well, Mr. Henry, it's nice to meet you."

"Ann, before we do any business, you and I, can I ask you a question?"

"Yes, of course."

"Tell me. How old are your daughters?"

She looked a little confused and said, "How did you know that I had daughters?"

"Well, I'm guessing you have two."

"You're right, but how do you know?"

"Oh, Ann, that's easy. You're wearing a necklace with birthstones. That's a dead giveaway that you have two girls. How old are they?"

"Well, the oldest one's 18, and the youngest one is 14."

"Ann, I have a 15-year-old daughter and an 11-year-old daughter. Any advice?"

"Prayer," she said. "Prayer is good."

"Well, we exercise that option."

She smiled. "You know, you're in a good mood. I'll bet you're going on vacation."

"No," I said. "I'm going to work. Mr. Karlson and I are going to Bermuda to do a conference, where I am going to speak."

"You're a speaker! What do you speak about, Mr. Henry?"

"I speak about service. It's one of those things I love to talk about."

"My favorite topic," she said.

"I had a feeling that you were going to say that."

"Mr. Henry, how can I help you?"

"Well, Ann, Mr. Karlson and I have tickets in different parts of the plane. I would like to sit with Mr. Karlson."

"Dr. Henry, this plane is oversold. There's absolutely no wiggle room."

"Ann, I know lots of things about you. The thing I know most about you is that you are a supervisor and a leader. If you can't get it done, then nobody can."

She said, "Let me try." She clicked the keys for a while and finally said, "Now, Mr. Henry, this will require you giving up your first-class seat."

"That's not a problem. I didn't pay for it. It was just out of the kindness of you folks from Delta that I received it."

"Is a bulkhead seat OK, right behind first class, for you and Mr. Karlson?"

"That's a wonderful place!"

She said, "I just moved around some folks who had e-tickets. I actually gave one of them a better seat."

As she handed me my boarding pass I said, "Your husband travels a lot, I would imagine."

"How would you know that?"

"All those charms from different parts of the country. Normally people don't buy themselves charms. Usually someone they love buys them."

She laughed. "You're right. Is there anything else I can do for you gentlemen?"

"Well, you know, we weren't able to check our luggage in Knoxville or Nashville, where we came from, because this is considered an international flight. Is there any way that you could perhaps check our luggage?"

"Of course we can." She looked at her watch. "You know, I'm getting off in five minutes. Why don't we just walk you down by the jetway and put your luggage by the plane so that it can be put into the baggage area?"

And we walked down and placed the luggage by the plane.

Ann laughed. "You know, this is silly. It's an hour before the plane leaves. It seems to me that you wanted to sit together because you wanted to talk, and it's awfully noisy up there. It's a pretty good walk to the Crown Room. Why don't I just go ahead and put you on the plane?"

We got comfortable in our seats, right behind first class. She told the flight attendants, "Ladies, these two gentlemen are my special guests. Anything they want, see that they get it."

I have acquired one interesting gift in my life from being an educator. That gift is good hearing. You tend to develop good hearing as a teacher. It helps you to interfere with any of the plotting that's going on in the back of the room. I could hear the flight attendants in the front of the plane having this conversation:

"Who are they?"

"I don't know, but they must be somebody, because nobody

gets on this plane while the cleanup crew is here. Nobody gets on this plane before first class."

A flight attendant walked back with a linen-covered tray like the ones they use in first class. "Can I get you gentlemen anything?" she asked.

"I would love some hot chocolate."

"I'll get it right away," she said. She asked Bill if he would like anything.

"Yes, I would like some hot chocolate as well."

When she came back and served us our hot chocolate, she looked at us and said, "Can I ask you something? Who are you?"

"Well, my name is Dale Henry. I am a speaker and trainer. This is Mr. Bill Karlson. He is also a speaker and runs a radio show out of Nashville, Tennessee, called *Making Top Dollar in a Job You Love*.

She nodded politely. "OK. Who are you, really?"

Again I said, "I am Dale Henry. I'm a speaker and a trainer. This is Mr. Bill Karlson. He runs a radio show."

She shrugged. "If you don't want to tell me, that's OK."

Let me tell you a little bit about our trip. We ate first-class food. (If you want to make people in coach upset, eat first-class food.) Every flight attendant on that plane knew our first names and called us by name whenever they served us. Incredible service! I would say better than first class, because we had become known.

As we neared Bermuda, Bill and I were talking about the concept. "Dale, this is phenomenal."

"No, it's not. You see, people treat people more kindly when they know who they are. We tend to treat our friends better than we treat people we don't know. We tend to treat people we like better than people we don't like. It's just common sense. Look, Bill, as powerful as becoming the known can be in a positive way, it can be just as powerful in a negative way. Play along with me."

In my briefcase I had a memento of a program I had done in Palm Springs, California, for the United States Marshals Service. They had given me one of their badges, one of their lapel pins. I pulled it out of my bag. When Mary, our first flight attendant, walked by, I smiled at her.

"Gentlemen, is there anything we can get you before we land?" she asked.

"Mary, you have been so kind to us and to all the other folks here on the plane. We feel a little guilty. I want to tell you who we really are."

She leaned down as if we were going to share a secret. "I won't tell anyone."

"My name is Dale Henry. I am a United States marshal. This man with me, Mr. Bill Karlson, is in my custody."

She nodded and left.

As you leave the plane after a flight, you are accustomed, no doubt, to having the airline personnel tell you how much they enjoyed having you aboard. As we made our way through first class all the flight attendants were lined up. I shook hands with them one by one. They called me by name, and I called them by name. The pilot stuck his head out of the cockpit to say hi to me as well. He knew my name too.

When Bill walked by, they all stepped back.

Become the known in a positive way. If you want to become the prize, you can't do it by passing the buck. You have to get past the excuses that keep you from excelling and accomplishing things that you want to do. You can do that through the power of your life and the way it is lived, and by letting others know the way you live it. Not by thumping on someone's head and trying to get them to do things the way you see they need to be done, but by quiet persuasion of the life you live. Zinging people not only with your ability to lead but also with your ability to follow.

By following God's example, become the perfect example and be His prize.

SECTION

5

ENERGIZE!

━ ━ ━ ━ ━ ━ ━ ━ ━ ━ ━ ━ ━ ━ ━ ━ ━ ━

13

Energize Yourself With Your Ability to Work With Others

Learning the lessons of teaming

―――――――

Whoever gives heed to instruction prospers.
—**PROVERBS 16:20.**

When it comes to working with others, people basically fall into two categories. There are people with whom you love to work, and customers and clients who make your life a joy. Then there are the other kind. You know the type—they tend to irritate you, to rub you the wrong way. I don't personally believe there are that many people on this planet whom we dislike. I do believe, however, that they move around a lot, so they tend to infect us all.

This chapter is about action and interaction with people, our ability to work well with some while being challenged by others. To be able to understand properly why some people are fun to work with and others aren't, we have to take a test. Many of you have taken all types of personality inventories. To be honest, they are all good. Mine is no better than the others—and no worse. However, the test is not what sets apart this inventory from others that also have ways of separating personalities. You've probably gotten information back from one of these tests only to find out that some of the things the test said about you were right, others not so right.

That's the reason it's so necessary that you follow one important bit of instruction when you take my test: I don't want you to think. For some of us, that won't be very difficult. For others it will be hard, because you will want to dissect everything down to its simplest component. You can't do that with this test. With this test we are looking for that knee-jerk reaction, that gut response. Before you look at the next page of the book, I want you to have a pencil ready and in your hand. You're going to see four lists of words. Each list is headed by a letter: T, E, A, and M. They mean absolutely nothing. They're simply ways of separating the four lists. There's no particular acronym that they spell. They are just four letters. Underneath each of the four letters, however, are 20 terms and phrases we are going to use to help you identify things about yourself.

Remember! No thinking—only gut response; just a knee-jerk reaction. I want you to be able to complete the list in less than a minute and a half. This is crucial! The quicker, the better. The faster you do it, the more accurate your personality inventory will be.

Here are the instructions once more:

You are going to look at the next page.

You will see four lists of words and phrases.

You will check off the words and phrases that apply to you. These words and phrases don't describe the way other people see you—they describe the way *you* see you. Check them off as quickly as possible.

Are you ready?

Team Profile
The Team and Systems Knowledge Profile

Instructions: Check each word or phrase that describes your individual traits. Total your check marks and multiply by 5. Circle the highest scoring letter.

T　　　E　　　A　　　M

T	E	A	M
❏ Likes Power	❏ Enthusiastic	❏ Loyal	❏ Accurate
❏ Takes Charge	❏ Takes Risks	❏ Calm	❏ Consistent
❏ Committed	❏ Visionary	❏ Nondemanding	❏ Controlled
❏ Secure	❏ Motivational	❏ Avoids Confrontations	❏ Reserved
❏ Solid	❏ Energetic	❏ Enjoys Routine	❏ Predictable
❏ Resourceful	❏ Highly Verbal	❏ Dislikes Change	❏ Orderly
❏ Competitive	❏ Promoter	❏ Warm and Relational	❏ Practical
❏ Enjoys Obstacles	❏ Friendly, Mixer	❏ Gives In	❏ Factual
❏ Problem Solver	❏ Enjoys Being Centered	❏ Indecisive	❏ Conscientious
❏ Goal Oriented	❏ Fun-Loving	❏ Dry Humor	❏ Perfectionist
❏ Decision Maker	❏ Likes Variety	❏ Adaptable	❏ Discerning
❏ Adventurous	❏ Spontaneous	❏ Sympathetic	❏ Detailed
❏ Strong Willed	❏ Enjoys Change	❏ Thoughtful	❏ Analytical
❏ Autonomous	❏ Group Oriented	❏ Nurturing	❏ Inquisitive
❏ Courageous	❏ Creative	❏ Patient	❏ Precise
❏ Controlling	❏ Optimistic	❏ Tolerant	❏ Persistent
❏ Persistent	❏ Initiator	❏ Good Listener	❏ Scheduled
❏ Action Oriented	❏ Humorous	❏ Peacemaker	❏ Sensitive
❏ Constructive	❏ Inspirational	❏ Sensitive Feelings	❏ Enjoys Instruction
❏ Determined	❏ Passionate	❏ Agreeable	❏ Fair

___TOTAL　　　___TOTAL　　　___TOTAL　　　___TOTAL

The scoring is very easy. Simply count the check marks in each of the four lists. The list with the most check marks indicates your personality type. Some of you may have the same number in two lists, and both are your high number. That's not unusual. What if you have three lists that have the same number? Don't worry. Even if you have the same number of check marks in all four lists, it's OK. It's probably because there are things happening in your life that are pulling you in about 10,000 different directions. Hopefully, after we finish describing the four TEAM categories and the way I see them, it will clear up some confusion.

Let's start with those who scored highest in the first list—the T people. Let me tell you a little bit about yourself. You are completers. You are goal setters. More than anything, however, you love the accomplishment of finishing. The chase means nothing to you. It's all about accomplishment. You don't like to dillydally. You don't like people who waste your time and slow you down. You hate that feeling of walking through mud. You like to get from point A to point B in a hurry. For that reason your motto is: "Do not tell me what to do."

Now, wait just a minute! Many of you T's are saying, "Aha! That's only the first half of the motto. The last half is: 'Tell me what you want done.'" You see, a T sees the world in this way: "Today I am at point A. Tomorrow I want to be at point B. There is one step between point A and point B."

Unfortunately, the whole world doesn't see things this way. The world sees the step from point A to point B with a hundred little steps in between. The T doesn't like that, because the T doesn't like instruction. They don't like to be told what to do, only what needs to be done. They are, as I said, completers.

When I was the dean of a college, I had an interesting secretary. Her habit was to come in early every day. She loved to come in early. She didn't have to be in until 8:00, but she was there at 7:30 every morning, checking the things that needed to be done and building a checklist that she could systematically go through and complete.

T's love to talk about their accomplishments. If you get three T's together, the conversation will go something like this:

"I got five projects done today," says one T.

"Well, that's nothing," the second T will say. "I got 10 projects done today."

The third T will laugh and say, "You guys must have taken breaks all day long, because I got 15 things done."

T's love the competition. They love to compete with everyone else, but mainly with other T's.

My secretary was a very high T. I'm not. Because of my particular personality trait, I love ritual. There are things I like to do because I like to do them. They give me pleasure. They make me feel good. Or I do them just because I do them. For example, almost every day I go to the restroom after lunch. It's what I do. It's a systematic thing for me, out of ritual, that I like to do after lunch. My secretary knew this.

One day in the early spring she walked over to the bathroom door and knocked. "Dr. Henry, are you in there?"

I said, "Yes."

"What are you doing?"

Some things should be self-evident. "I'm in the restroom, Betty."

"I know you are in the restroom, Dr. Henry, but where are you exactly?"

"Betty, I'm in the stall."

I was 41 years old at the time, and in that 41 years I'd seen lots of things in the bathroom. But I had never seen a pair of black pumps. Under the door of the stall was a pair of black pumps. Connected to the person in those black pumps was a hand that reached under the door of the stall, holding a sheet of paper.

"Sign this," Betty instructed. "I need it now."

Since I was the dean of a college, my mind immediately began to race. This must be urgent! No doubt some poor student had messed up and was being kicked out of our college, or had gotten in trouble with their financial aid and needed help. That's what deans do. We fight the good fight.

I looked at this piece of paper and couldn't believe my eyes. It was the invoice for the potato chip man. I thought, *I'm not going to sign the invoice for the potato chip man while my secretary waits outside the stall in the men's restroom.* That's when I remembered that she was a T, and if I didn't sign it, she would just come in and get it. So I signed it and handed it back under the door.

She left, whistling. Why? Because she was happy. That was one more thing she could check off her list, one more detail completed. What T's hate more than anything on the planet is the wasting of their time. They say "Well, I don't have time for that" or "That's a waste of my time" to do that activity. They love talking about time, but not in the way most of us relate to it. They talk about time because they wanted everything yesterday. Completion of the task is the most important thing to the T.

Maybe you're thinking, *This is interesting, but isn't this just a developmental thing all of us go through?* I don't think so. I've been an educator all my life. I know developmental things when I see them. Our personalities are not developmental. Our personalities are as much us as our fingerprints and that reflection we see in the mirror.

I live in a wonderful family. We have a very simple rule in my house that stems from the fact that I am an only child. Growing up without any siblings, I became a bit shy. When most people hear that, they say, "Dale, you stand in front of hundreds of thousands of people every year and speak. How can you be shy?"

It's very simple. I have my clothes on when I speak. I am shy when I don't have any clothes on. I married a wonderful woman, but unfortunately (or fortunately, whichever way you choose to see it), when you get married, your spouse is going to see you without any clothes on. I got used to that over a 12-year period.

And then we had children. Small children who walk around, point, and ask questions. So I developed a rule in my house. It's a simple rule—nothing complicated. The rule is this: While I am taking a shower, don't come into the bathroom. This isn't a difficult rule. Once about every six months or so, I sit everyone down and we talk about this rule.

I look at LeAnne and say, "LeAnne, what is my rule?"

"Don't go into the bathroom while you are taking a shower."

"Right, LeAnne; that's exactly right."

"Lauren, what is the rule?"

"Don't go in the bathroom while you are taking a shower."

"Good."

"Unless it's an emergency," Lauren adds.

"No, no. See, there's no emergency. If the house is on fire, I'm in water."

This is a waste of my time. Lauren is a T. She believes that from point A to point B is merely a step. It's not a process. Telling her that she can't do it means only that she must find a way to do it. Therein lies the problem.

A couple of years ago I was taking a shower. I was enjoying my shower. It's one of those things that wakes me up in the morning. It gets me going, gets my blood pumping. And it's something I also do in the evening to relax. I was enjoying my shower when I heard the bathroom door open, the bathroom door that was locked. My baby, Lauren, was born with a straight piece of metal behind her ear that will pop one of those keyless locks open in half a heartbeat. There she stood, wrapped in a towel, looking me in the eye.

"Lauren," I said. "What's the rule?"

"The rule is, Dad, don't come in the bathroom while you are taking a shower unless it's an emergency, and this is an emergency."

"What is the nature of your emergency?"

"My Barbie is drowning."

To an adult male's way of thinking, that is not an emergency. An emergency is stepping on a Barbie at night. But to a small girl, that's an emergency.

"Well, what do you want me to do?"

"I need my Barbie boat."

"OK. Do you know where your Barbie boat is?"

"Yes, Daddy, it's downstairs, either on the inside or the outside of the garage door. It's one or the other, Dad."

"If you know where it is, Lauren, why don't you go get it?"

"Because it's dark, Dad."

I remembered being small, and I was empathetic. "OK. You go back to your bathroom, and I'll go get Barbie's boat for you."

We have a sense of humor in my house that revolves around the way we like to tease each other. My family had bought me a terry cloth robe that I liked very much. Unfortunately, because of their twisted sense of humor, they bought it at a big-and-tall men's shop. Have I mentioned that I'm five feet six? I am neither big nor tall. When I wear this robe, it has a train. But that's not the problem. Actually, a train is good. I can cover up my feet. The problem, though, is with the sash, which was made for a man with girth. So I have to tie this sash into a lump the size of a football around my waist.

So I got out of the shower and tied my sash into the football knot. I had started to walk down the steps when it occurred to me that if I grabbed my garage door opener from the key rack next to the door, I could walk down and hit the garage door opener. Even if the Barbie boat was on the outside of the garage, I could easily pick it up and take it back upstairs and be back in the shower before I even dried off.

I grabbed the garage door opener and put it in the front pocket of my robe. When I opened the laundry room door that leads into the garage, the garage lights shone brightly on the Barbie boat, lying up against the garage door. On a trip to the beach I had hurt my back. My doctor recommended that I squat more instead of bending over. I decided that this was a good time to practice my squat. So I leaned against the garage door and squatted down to pick up the Barbie boat.

This action of squatting set off a series of events. The weight against my robe pocket activated the garage door opener, and the garage door began to open, snagging the back of my robe. When it snagged the back of my robe, I wasn't fully aware that my robe had been snagged until that first cool breeze blew in under the door. By the time I realized the door was going up while I was squatting down, it was too late. You do the math. The door is nine feet tall. I'm five feet six.

Hanging from the garage door on my tiptoes, I discovered an amazing thing. How quickly the mind works! In that split second of hanging there, my mind reminded me that it was about the time of night when my neighbors walk, small children ride their bikes, and women walk their dogs. All I could think was *You're going to jail, Dale.* I didn't want to go to jail, so I started working on that football knot, which was now firmly positioned in my armpit. As I was working on it (which probably took less than 20 seconds to undo), my thoughts turned to the day's events.

For four months my wife had been bugging me to replace the light in the garage. I had done it that day. Not with a regular 60-watt bulb, of course, but with a 100-watt bulb. Now my shadow was cast across three of my neighbors' yards. All I could think about was my neighbors, positioned on the back steps of their porches, their VCR cameras in the on position, exclaiming, "Ten thousand dollars, you are mine!"

I finally freed myself of that robe and, sliding down, grabbed Barbie's boat, which by now was a blessing in its new role as a loincloth. I shut the door—and started laughing. I believe that true humor is tragedy plus time. Sometimes in the grip of a situation we say, "Well, we'll laugh about this someday." Why wait? Why not laugh now? It's funny.

I met Debra (who is not a T) at the top of the stairs. "What are you laughing at?" she demanded.

"Well," I said, "I went downstairs to get Lauren's Barbie boat. When I squatted down, I set off the garage door opener in my pocket, and the garage door, on its way up, snagged the back of my—"

"You weren't naked!" she cried in alarm.

"Well, not totally. My head was covered up."

"Oh, dear, don't worry," she soothed. "It's a very dark night. There isn't even a moon out."

"Maybe not from where you were standing," I said darkly. "But from where I was standing, believe me, darling, there was a full moon."

How did I get in this position? Very simply, because a T wanted something *now*. Immediately, not later. T's want resolution. They want time to be on their side, because they like to take charge. They are resourceful folks, courageous and constructive but very determined.

Now let's look at the E category. If you have more check marks in the E category, that means your motto is: "It's easier to get forgiveness than to ask permission." You are a chameleon. No, I don't mean one of those lizards lying on a limb. You like to pretend that you are other people.

Amazingly, you like to pretend that you are T's. The best thing I can tell you is that you are never going to be a T, because E's aren't completers. E's are dreamers. E's are big-picture people. I mean *big* picture. We can see it, but we're not going to paint it. We just see it. We plant the seed and move along. We're the Johnny Appleseed of personalities. We love to talk.

I love to catch E's in the act of pretending to be T's. Usually it happens in a break room or where there are lots of people. T's will be standing around talking about accomplishments and what they've been able to finish during the day, you know, the "I-got-five-things-done," "I-got-10-things-done," "I-got-15-things-done" conversation. At that very moment that E will walk up and say, "Yeah, me too."

Unfortunately, E's, you haven't really accomplished that much, at least in measurable things. Oh, your accomplishments are many. You are information giants. Let me tell you how that happens. You probably get memos where you work. E's don't read memos. When an E receives a memo in their box, they immediately go to everybody else in that office, waving the memo, and say, "Hey, have you seen this yet? What does that say to you?" From there, they move from person to person, waving the memo saying, "Hey!" and gathering information. At the end of the day they will know more about that memo than anybody else in the organization.

And you know what? They never read it, because they get the

information from you. They are able to glean not only the information that was in the memo, but also what you know about it, and they store it.

I love to watch E's do e-mail. E's will compose that e-mail and hit the "send" key. If that e-mail is going to somebody on the same floor, they will jump up, run to that person, and say, "Hey, did you get my e-mail?" If the e-mail recipient is in an office across town or across the street, they hit the send button, then pick up the phone and say, "Hey! Did you get my e-mail?"

Sending the e-mail means nothing to the E. They want to know what you think. They want to hear your reaction. Most of all, they want to see your face, because they can read you like a book. The E has power through information. They are enthusiastic. They are passionate, but at the same time they are often procrastinators. Don't take this the wrong way. The E is a viable component to the team and the organization because they sell the concept. The T couldn't get anything done if it weren't for the E out there, promoting and selling the concept. Remember, they aren't painters; they're dreamers. Dreams don't happen without dreamers. E's are fun-loving people. They love to talk. They love to laugh. They like to be the center of the conversation. They like attention. The E has lots of energy.

A's are an interesting group. What makes them interesting, at least to me, is the fact that they're hard to figure. First, let me tell you a little bit about A's. Have you ever heard someone say, "They hold their nose against the grindstone"? That describes A's. They're go-getters, pleasers. They love to complete a task because it gives them self-worth.

Interestingly enough, though, A's do the strangest thing. Have you ever said something to somebody and then see them go somewhere? You know, like in their head? Usually the look is distant, like they're staring off toward the horizon. The reason A's do that a lot is that they're asked from time to time, "What do you think about that?" Don't expect an A to answer that. They can't, because to tell you what they think would be to break their code. These are the people who truly believe in the adage "If you can't say something nice, don't say anything at all."

If you want to get a true reading of an A, do what the E's do. When an E talks to an A, they don't say, "What do you think about that?" They say, "Well, how do you feel about that?" You will get a response to that, because the A's life rotates around and is immersed in *feeling*. An A will tell you how they feel and how the people around them feel. They equate success with this feeling.

We now see the first problem of interaction. It's between A's and T's. T's aren't real fond of A's, because T's don't like to give instruction or take instruction. On the other hand, A's love instruction. They want you to tell them what needs to be done and how it needs to be done so that they can complete the task exactly to your specification. Then you will see them as an esteemed person. They get esteem by seeing you and watching you tell them how much you enjoyed the completion of that project.

T's won't do that. T's won't hand you a project and start telling you what they want. T's will merely tell you what they need done. Now, this is an A nightmare. The A does not want to do the one step. They like all those little steps between point A and point B. But the T isn't going to do that. Because of the frustration this sets up—when the A asks for more information and the T refuses to give it—they see it as locking horns. Both parties believe the other is not giving them what they need.

"You're putting me in mud," says T.

"You're not sharing information," retorts A.

The M does get along with the T. The M likes the fact that the T is going to get it done. The T likes the fact that the E moves a little faster, without asking for any more information. Why? Because the E already *knows* the information. E has basically talked to everybody in the organization and knows what's going on.

The A's, though, feel as if they are on an island. They feel as though T is pulling the boat away without giving them any kind of direction on how to get back to the mainland. This frustrates them.

The E sees this from both points of view. Why? Because the E gets along with the A's, as well. Strangely enough, if you are an E, when you get through reading this book you will probably want to look at your spouse or those people with whom you get along fabulously, and you'll probably find out that they are A's. E's and A's get along great because E's love to talk and A's love to listen.

Even though the A's sound like wonderful people, they do have a flaw. This flaw happens during stress, during the time that the T's are giving them projects to complete without the proper information to complete them. They literally waste days doing a project that would have taken an hour to complete if they had been provided with the proper information. They will get it done, though, because the completion of the project is somehow tied to their esteem.

This friction between the T and the A does not go unnoticed by the A. Remember, however, that their personality will not allow them to say anything—at first. Oh, you T's can rub an A the wrong way 10 times, maybe even 20, 30, or 50 times, but there will come a fifty-first time. It will usually be a little thing, maybe a bent paper clip. But it sets them off. When that happens, you don't want to be there. It's a bit like standing at ground zero during an atomic blast. You are going to get taken out.

You see, the A will explode. During that explosion they will tell you everything you did to them during the past 15 years, in chronological order, and there's not much you can say, because it's all the truth. They have very good memories, and usually (I want to make sure you understand this "usually") this aggression is not aimed at the E, because the E is the A's best friend. But if you happen to be there at ground zero, well, when they get done with the T you're next.

I don't like being next. Usually I can tell when my wife is upset with my daughters. If I can hear that they are having a conflict, I know to leave, because I know that in just a few minutes that wonderful wife of mine—that A, so sweet, so wonderful—is going to come downstairs, and I'm going to be next.

Years and years of experience have taught me and other E's how to escape this conflict. Here's what you must do. As the A comes in, wagging that finger and telling you what has just happened and why it's your fault, you wait for the pause. Lots of times this can be a lengthy wait, because the A's can talk while they're inhaling. It's something to see. But eventually they do inhale, and they do pause.

When that happens, stand up, stick your finger out, point it into their face and say, "You are exactly right!"

They will come back with "You'd better believe I'm right!" but it will make them lose their place. They'll usually leave the room mumbling, "Well, there was something else, but I can't remember what it was." You have escaped by the skin of your teeth. Because you're an E, you are a survivor. But sometimes you get trapped.

A's believe that in their E spouse's knee is a mute switch, and, when it is grasped, it sends a signal that states, "You know, you might just want to be quiet." Then the signal travels up to the eyes. My wife will look at me, and I can see this message flashing in her eyes: "If you want to have as much fun as you have had so far, you might want to keep your mouth shut."

We E's have some problems too. When we get stressed we say things we really don't mean. You see this in life's little last-nerve things. Some people drive their cars goofy. E's talk to people who drive their cars goofy. My dad, who is the world's biggest E, talks to people who drive their cars goofy. If someone pulls over on him, they are an idiot. If someone pulls in front of him, that person is an idiot. If he pulls out in front of someone else, that person is an idiot.

Dad once drove my girls to school for two weeks. The first time we drove together after they returned, they asked, "Dad, where are all the idiots today?"

I said, "Well, I think they are with your grandfather."

We E's talk only to people in other cars. The reason this happens is that the E engages their brain about 30 seconds after they engage their mouth, and that gets them into trouble sometimes. That's why an A grabs an E's leg. They know that mute switch must be engaged.

My wife and I were on a cruise, enjoying our meal with another couple. I was enjoying a conversation with a wonderful woman across the table from me when she got that "look." I don't know any other way to describe it.

She said, "Do you know what's driving me crazy about this cruise?"

"No." Before I could say anything else, my wife's hand went under the table, grabbed my knee, and squeezed. I knew that was my cue to be quiet. This cruise had been fun, and if I wanted it to continue being fun, I would shut up.

The woman continued. "What really drives me nuts on this cruise is Where do they get the electricity for the ship?"

Ladies and gentlemen, I am an E. My purpose in life is to point out stupidity. When I see stupidity, I want to stomp it out like a fire. My wife knows that, and that is why her hand was on my knee, gently squeezing it. I wanted to comment. I wanted to look across the table and say, "Ma'am, they make the electricity on the ship. You don't see an extension cord stretching from Miami, Florida, to the ship, do you?" But I couldn't. My mute switch had been turned on.

The pain on my face must have told her that, and, like a shark, she sensed the blood in the water. "As much as that bothers me, though, what really kills me are the people who work on the ship. Where do they sleep?"

My foot was almost asleep from the pressure that my wife was exerting on my knee. I wanted to respond to this question by saying, "They sleep on the ship! You haven't seen anybody jump off every eight hours, have you? There's no barge behind the ship that they swim to at bedtime. Your waiter isn't wet."

My wife looked serenely at the woman and said, "I don't have a clue." That's what A's do.

I thought I had survived the meal. I thought I was going to make it OK. I bit my tongue many times, not to mention my cheek. I was proud of myself.

That's when she hit me with her best shot. That's when she delivered the killer punch. That's when she said, "What really bothers me is this: How far above sea level do you think we are right now?"

Oh, you E's out there! You know the answer that trembled on the tip of my tongue. You are screaming it right now. I wanted so badly to say, "We're floating on it." But I didn't, because my best friend is an A, and I knew it would break her heart. It didn't do much for my blood pressure, but I lived through it.

About now the T's are feeling a little self-righteous. They're saying, "You E's and you A's, you get all stressed out because you are people persons. That doesn't stress me. Oh, when you get stressed, T's, you are amazingly funny. You talk to your furniture. You stand at a file drawer, looking in it, making such comments as "I can't believe these people who work with me!" Talking into a file drawer. Pretty strange. I tell you this because if you're walking down the hall and see a T talking to their file cabinet, it might be a good idea to come back later.

T's, E's, and A's. What have we learned so far? T's and A's don't get along. Why? Because T's don't like instruction, and A's do. E's and T's get along; E's and A's get along, but T's and A's don't.

That leaves us with the M's, whose motto is: "If you aren't going to do it right, don't do it at all." These are the people who walk around in your organization, day in and day out, looking at the floor or at some piece of paper they are carrying, saying, "If it weren't for me, we'd all be in jail." They are the rule keepers. They are the fair givers. They try to make sure that if somebody gets something, everybody does. If one person doesn't get it, the rest of us don't get it either. Fairness is their byword.

Let me give you a rundown of the problem this we-are-the-only-people-who-do-things-right thinking creates. This is a mindset. Among T's, E's, and A's, which category would you think has the lowest heart attack rate and stress on the planet?

It's the A's. They won't hold on to stress. They'll take it for a while; then they will explode.

The E's don't have a lot of stress, because they pretty much blow up when something happens that they don't like. They are communicators and talkers. They don't have any problem doing this.

T's don't have stress—they give it.

We come now to the M's, the most stressed people of the four categories, the group that has the highest rate of heart attacks and strokes. These people tend to carry it inside them. They have a hard time walking away from a closet that's messy. They see something that needs to be done, and they do it before they go on to the next thing, thus causing more and more stress. The stress builds because each thing requires more time. Theirs is almost a compulsive need to get things right.

Male T's, if you have folding money in your pocket or wallet, it's probably separated by denomination, and each bill is turned the same way.

I love the M's, but, if you've noticed that the T's and A's don't get along, you will also notice that the E's and M's don't get along either. It's because of their mottoes. An E believes it's easier to get forgiveness than permission. An M believes that if you aren't going to do it right, don't do it at all.

An M will actually walk into a room, see an E doing something, and say, "Hey, you can't do that!"

"Why not?" the E responds.

The M will counter, "Because Mr. Johnson said you can't do it."

"Well," says E, "Mr. Johnson isn't here, is he?"

This drives M nuts.

It works the other way, too. I don't know why, but it seems that every M on the planet is in charge of the copy machine. A million times a day E's have to listen to M's say, as they walk out of the copy machine room, arms over their heads, "Am I the only person who puts paper in the copy machine?"

Of course, the E's are the ones who always break the copy machine. We'll be in there, toner up to both elbows, pulling out paper, because that's what we've always done before, and the M will walk in and say, "What are you doing to my copy machine?"

Of course, it's theirs. It belongs to them because they put paper in it all the time. "Did you read the instructions?" they will say.

"There are instructions?" E asks, because no one has told them.

M's and E's stress each other out. We are as much enemies as are T's and A's. For this reason, I've always tried to get along with my M brothers and sisters. Sometimes it's tough. My registrar in college was an M, a rule follower. I actually have been told by this person that a fax is not real.

"You can touch it," I pointed out. "You can see it."

"But it has no stamp on it," she countered. "Therefore, it is not real."

I struggled with this person, trying my best to build a relationship, trying to get along with her. And I thought I was making some headway. I took her out to lunch one day. We were enjoying a conversation on the way back from our favorite restaurant, walking across the parking lot. Then this person stopped, cleaned off a 10-foot circle, and threw a fit.

"This is the reason you can't find a parking space on this campus," she ranted. "It's because of idiots like this who take up more than one parking space."

It was my car she was looking at. This all stems from the fact that E's and M's park differently. An E will zip into a parking lot, tires screeching, and pull into a spot. He could care less if he's inside or outside a parking space. The important thing is that he's there, maybe even early. An M, though, will pull into a parking space and raise himself up with his steering wheel, trying to see if he fits perfectly between the two lines. If not, he backs up, realigns himself— even gets out of the car and looks to make sure the car is perfectly positioned between the two white lines. The E's would have forgotten why they were there if they took that much time to park.

M's are fair people. But do we need them? Yes! I've often heard people say, "If we were more alike, the world would be easier. It would be a more livable place." Would it? What would it be like if we were all T's? Miserable! We would all be rushing about, getting things done.

How about E's? Well, it would be different. We'd probably

work one day a week, and it would be dress-down day.

A's? Maybe the world would be better if we were all A's, but it would be boring.

And M's? Well, everything would be right, but who would care? It would always be right. There would be nobody there to stir everything up, nobody to create chaos and change. I like chaos. I'm an E. M's don't like chaos. For that reason, we don't agree.

But can we agree on this? It's not our *alikeness* that makes us strong. It's our *diversity* that makes us rich. If you're thinking that you can't go into your organization and present this test so that you can figure out who's what and know how to work with them, here's what can you do.

Listen to conversations. The T's will talk about how important it is to get things done. They are always pushing, taking the road not necessarily less traveled, but the one with the quickest path.

E's love to talk, converse, question. "Why?" they will say. "Why not?"

A's. You know these people. When you come to work in the morning, they want to know how you are, and they are serious. They are empathetic. They are wonderful people to work with, the backbone of every team, the glue that holds us together. They are caregivers.

We have to have the M's, because without them we would be in chaos. There would be nobody following rules. The only rule would be that there are none. A society cannot function in that way.

As we end this chapter, let's go to a boardroom. It's a budget meeting. People are surrounding the table, paperwork in hand. Watch them carefully. The T will fold that sheet so that only the bottom line can be seen. If it's good, the T will nod yes. If it's bad, he will shake his head no and cut to the chase—the solution. "What do we need to do?" is what the T wants to know.

Watch E's. They will lean to the left or the right, paper in hand, and ask their neighbors, "What is this?" They want that verbal communication. They could care less about paper. They want interaction.

Sometime during that meeting the A will hold up the report and say, "Who typed this? This is the best-looking report we have had all year, and I love this paper!" They are always building esteem.

The M will say nothing, because he's reading the report. "Second paragraph," he will say. "Third word. Misspelled. Has anybody run a calculator on these numbers?" M's want it right, and rightly so, because it's their nature.

God made each of us and gave us gifts. Not to use them would be a crime. But to question others' gifts might be an even bigger crime. Love those around you because they are like you. Love those around you because they are not, and be thankful.

14

Energize Your Witness

How to become the master ship builder.

A wicked messenger falls into trouble, but a trustworthy envoy brings healing.—PROVERBS **13:17**.

I like to browse. Since I was a little boy I've always liked looking at things, trying to decide if I'd like to take them home. During a visit to a hobby shop not too long ago, I observed a kit that would enable one to build a ship in a bottle. I asked the clerk if he sold many.

"I've sold a few, but I doubt very seriously that many of them have been put together."

I thought that was strange, so I asked him why he would say such a thing.

Without looking up, he replied, "It takes too long."

With those words fresh in my brain I made my way to a shady spot where I could relax and wait for my family to finish their shopping. That's when I met a most interesting man. He was leaning back on a park bench with his cap pulled slightly over his eyes. "Have a seat," he invited. "Don't mind me. I'm just waiting for my ship to come in."

I had just seen a project that no one wanted because it took too much time. Now here was a fellow waiting on an event that would likely never happen. What an interesting paradox!

That did it. On my way home I started scribbling down words that ended with "ship." There are quite a few, I discovered. The more words I wrote, the more I thought of. The more I thought of, the more I saw the power of the ship. Regardless of the word, when you add "ship" you take the concept to the next level. It's one thing to be a leader, but it's something else to be involved in the act of leadership.

In this chapter we're going to look at some ships, some vessels, that will allow ordinary people to do extraordinary things with their lives, essentially turning them into ship builders. This chapter isn't about building ships, but about building character with our abilities to lead. The concept is quite old. To be able to lead, you must possess the proper tools. As I travel I meet lots of people who are waiting for their ships to come in. That's just it—they wait and wait. I like what my grandfather told me when I was a boy. "Son, you have to send a few ships out before you can expect one to come in."

Stewardship. One of my favorite ships is stewardship, how we take care of our money and how we choose to spend it. To be a good steward, to ride this steward ship that we are talking about, you have to understand that something on sale isn't a deal unless you need it. In this country we take our shopping seriously. Sam Walton made a fortune by selling things with smiley faces on them, convincing us that we couldn't live without them. I'm pretty sure that life is not a race to see who can accumulate the most useless stuff.

We can always think of a reason to spend money. We have all kinds of experts advising us on what we can't live without. We have to smell good, they say. So we buy cologne and deodorant. Then they tell us we have to look good. So we buy designer clothes with fancy names plastered all over the back. We have to ride in style, so we go into debt to buy what everybody else is driving. Ninety-nine times out of a hundred, it's stuff we wouldn't have been caught dead in three years ago.

Why do we buy stuff that stresses us? That's simple. Sooner or later you have to pay the fiddler. Most of the time, disagreements between married couples are over money. "Where did it go?" he'll ask. "Don't blame me!" she counters. "You're the one who couldn't live without the new bass boat in the driveway!" And whoa, Nellie! The fur flies! I'm talking about a real slobber knocker. The stress builds until someone says something that crushes someone they love very much. Sound familiar? Financial stress is something we all have dealt with at one time or another.

I can remember a time my child bride and I had plenty of month left over at the end of our money. That's why I always have the rule that if you've got so much stuff that you have to rent storage space, you've got too much stuff. The problem with buying stuff you really don't need is just that—you really don't need it. Debra and I have been accumulating this stuff we are talking about for more than 27 years.

We bought a new house about three years ago, and we decided to simplify. Our dilemma is that my wife is a retired elementary school teacher, and we have conflicting philosophies. She believes that you should never throw anything away that you can stack up. My philosophy has always been that when in doubt, pitch it out. So what happened? Well, at first I won out. Only the items that we really needed were brought to the new house.

As the years have gone by, little by little, most of the stack-up stuff has made its way into the new ponderosa, proving the adage that if mama ain't happy, ain't nobody happy. We have all heard that a fool and his money are soon parted. My shop teacher in high school gave me some great advice. (Who else would cut off his own finger just to use it as a safety lecture?) He said, "Never argue with a fool, because it's impossible for those listening to determine which person has any sense."

When we get stressed over money, we've lost every bit of our good sense. It's a lot like fussing over who let the cow out of the barn instead of going out and finding her. I ran into a great sign in a friend's office. It states, "Bring your troubles right on in, just as long as you accompany them with some solutions."

So here are my solutions to stressing over money. We can call them Dale's Stewardship Advice. If you're fighting over money, stop, and start managing it. Nothing is that important. When you see something you can't live without, try living without it for 10 days. If, after 10 days, you still have a pulse, you didn't need it that badly. Before buying a big-ticket item, go out and rent one for a while. Maybe your desire will flatten long before your wallet does. Plan long-term financial goals with your loved ones. The family that saves together, well, they eat regularly. Remember the golden rule of buying new vehicles: the new wears off long before the payment book wears out. An old proverb says: "A stitch in time saves nine." (It makes you wonder what could be done with a good sewing machine.) If the two of you can't agree on buying something, it's a sure sign that you aren't going to enjoy owning it.

Friend, when it comes to stewardship, we have to be smart. We have to stop working for our money and start making our money work for us. You can't do that until you stop stealing. Most of us have stolen at one time or another. Oh, I'm not talking about the garden variety of thief who goes and breaks into a store. I'm talking about stealing what belongs to God. God's part, the best part, the first part. The firstfruits, that 10 percent. Be a steward. Build a steward ship in your life. This first ship, this first building block, will cause your life to be more enriched and will give you an opportunity to show where your priority is in giving to God.

Relationship. Our next important ship is a friend ship. Relationships are important. Keeping those friends close to you is even more important.

Once I was sitting in a high school study hall, reading a science book. I must have read the same chapter 10 times, and one part of it at least 15 times. There was a pretty girl sitting next to me in study hall. She looked at me and smiled and said, "Are you having trouble reading that chapter?"

What made this really tough was that I was a junior and she was a freshman. Everybody who knows anything knows that when a freshman asks a junior if they are having trouble reading, that's embarrassing. I wasn't having trouble reading. I read just fine. The problem wasn't reading; it was comprehending. I told her I could read the chapter, but I couldn't remember anything the chapter said.

She leaned over the table. "You know, when I read a chapter that's really tough, I usually wait until I get home so that I can read it out loud."

That made some sense. So that night I read that chapter aloud in my bedroom. I got it the first time. I may not have done too many things in my life that were very smart, but what I did with my relationship with that young girl in study hall was pure genius. I ended up marrying her. We have had a relationship that has spanned more than 30 years. Looking back on that relationship, I don't think I would change a thing. She's my best friend, and I love her very much. Our life together has been nothing but a joy.

Relationships are important. But why we get into them is just as important. To maintain my sanity, I have what I refer to as a three-tiered leadership plan. This leadership plan circulates around the idea of relationships. I try to position myself on the second tier. On the step below me, I try to keep a number of people whom I am mentoring, people I try to share with and help become better. One step above me, I put people I call stretchers. Stretchers cause me to want to be better. On many occasions the mentorees, who are one step below me, are also stretchers, and I move them back and forth from the bottom step to the top step.

This may sound a little complicated to you, but it works for me. I believe all of us need people in our lives who will help us improve. By the same token, teaching someone else this method that we have just learned will stretch not only us, but also the people we are mentoring.

One such stretching occurred in Florida. Lauren and I had some time together and decided to spend the day at you-know-where—Mickey's place. Even though it was the middle of summer and a particularly hot day, we were having a wonderful time. We found ourselves in the middle of a large group of people, working our way toward a ride I really didn't want to go on. But Lauren did. After almost an hour we were almost to the head of the line. Lauren looked up at me and said, "Daddy, I'm sick." Inches away from our primary goal, we turned back.

We threaded our way through the people maze, back to the entrance. I fanned her with the map that Disney had given us to find our way through the theme park. As I stood there fanning my daughter, doing the only thing I knew to do to cool her off, the young woman who was running one of the small vending stands came to me with a cold bottle of water. "Here, this will help her cool down."

My automatic knee-jerk response as a dad was to put my hand in my pocket and get money out to pay for the water. This young woman looked at me and said, "Oh, no; the water is on the Mouse," and walked away. I suddenly found myself on that middle step, being stretched by a young woman who had taught me a great principle. That's when I noticed I wasn't on the second step anymore. I was on the bottom step, as a mentoree. This woman had assumed the middle position on the three steps. I saw her as a stretcher, but she was really the mentor. The stretcher was across the street.

As the young woman walked back to her stand, I caught sight of a young man selling snow cones and ice-cold slushees. He had taken in the whole scene, and he started to applaud. He clapped. This kind of blew me away. After I was sure my daughter was cooled off and feeling better, I walked over because I wanted to make sure that I understood the lesson I had received. I told the young man that what he had done was nothing short of amazing. His answer will stay with me for the rest of my life. It will help me as I build my relationships with Debra, LeAnne, Lauren, my parents, those people I am mentoring, and those folks I look up to for stretching.

He said, "Sir, we all need a little encouragement from time to time. I just wanted to show that young woman how amazing her act really was." Building relationships is pretty powerful.

Friendship. Our third ship is that ship we call the friend ship. We had just returned from a vacation in Florida, where we'd had a lot of fun. December is a great time to spend a week in Florida, a good time to escape the cold winter of eastern Tennessee.

While I was gone I was thinking about this chapter on friendships. When I got home I picked up a fax from the machine, expecting something there from a client, or maybe some Christmas wishes. Instead, it was from my secretary and office manager, Michelle Nail (who is also a travel agent). It needs to go in this chapter because it's a great reminder of how important giving to others, building friendship, really is. The letter goes like this:

"Dear Dr. Dale,

"As I am helping you type your story to the world, I have one of my own that I know only you would understand. I was standing outside last night before going to bed. I heard my wind chimes singing, which is unusual for this time of year, especially since there was no wind last night. Those wind chimes usually get on my last nerve. I don't like the sound of them because they are metal, and I have thought often of taking them down. But last night I heard them, and they played a beautiful melody, almost like an old song that you've heard before but had long forgotten. It was like something out of an old movie, like *Casablanca*.

"When I heard them I immediately looked over my shoulder where they swayed and thought, *There must be an angel present.* In my mind I said, 'Hello, angel! Thank you for coming to see me tonight. You must be cold. Come in and stay with us tonight, and make yourself at home.'

"I've often heard that when you hear wind chimes, there is an angel present, as George Bailey told his daughter in *It's a Wonderful Life,* but I've never once thought that when I heard my own chimes. To be honest, I've never heard wind chimes and felt a presence of any kind. Like I said, they usually aggravate me. I thought, *Well, maybe I just think that it's an angel because it's Christmas and joy is in the air. Maybe I am just in a holiday spirit.* God and I are good friends, and I can usually tell when He's got something to say to me, because He lets me know it's Him, somewhere in the back of my mind. I respond to it automatically, as if He taps me on the shoulder.

"This morning I got a call from the daughter of one of my clients. She was calling for her mother, Carolyn Chester, to tell me that Sylvia Templeton, Carolyn's best friend, had died last night in her sleep. In April Carolyn, Sylvia, and I had gone on a cruise together. Sylvia and I spent one night talking about our husbands. She said, 'Michelle, my husband was the love of my life.'

"Sylvia wasn't a spring chicken, but she certainly was active for a woman in her 70s. Carolyn told me today that Sylvia had sent her a travel kit for Christmas and that they were planning their next trip. As you know, my clients are not just clients—they are friends.

"I was remembering Sylvia and what a good time she had had on her last trip with me. If you ever look at your life's work and wonder if it made a difference to anyone, I'm here to tell you that it matters not only in our lives but also in those we touch.

"Being a travel agent is often a thankless job because of circumstances out of your control, but I did it because I like to help people. Sometimes you hear so much negativity that you think you don't make a difference, and you get tired of trying to help people. But you trudge on because it's your nature. And one day, when you're not looking, you find out that your efforts made all the difference in the world to that one person, and it makes it all seem worth the trouble.

"Merry Christmas."

Michelle had discovered what a lot of people discover. Friendship isn't what someone gives you. Friendship is something you must ride on together. It requires you to send that ship out so that one will come back.

Many years ago when we were newlyweds Debra and I moved into a subdivision. I noticed a neighbor was tilling his garden. It was dreadfully hot, and he went inside to cool off. I had just purchased a new riding lawn mower that had a tiller attachment. So I hooked it up, went next door, and finished the job. As I started to drive away Mr. Cochran came out to thank me. He said, "You know what? A friend ain't worth much until you need one."

He was right. Friends aren't friends unless they are there when you need them. Cultivation of good friends is difficult, but the fruit of that friendship is everlasting.

Championship. The fourth and final ship we will build together is our champion ship. I have personally never approved of calling leaders winners. I guess my logic presumes that to be a winner you must constantly win. If you lose, well, you can't be a winner. Being a champion suggests that you have succeeded as a leader. Let me explain why I think this is so powerful.

If you consider the odds, all of us lose more times than we win. Practice doesn't make you perfect. Repetition alone tends to make you mediocre. The more we do something, the more automatic it becomes. Look at those things you do best, a talent you have, a certain skill. Will practice make you better? Will it make you more passionate? Probably not.

To make the transition from amateur or winner to champion involves a shift in the way we think. A champion must be willing to learn from both successes and failures. In doing so, the champion discovers that winning is not the best teacher. The best lessons come from losses. These losses hone our skills much faster than successes. Winning is a tricky thing. You might not win because you are good. You might have won because your competition was lousy. Winning seduces us into thinking we are much better than we actually are. Leadership is built on a solid foundation of experiences. Being a winner suggests someone who is living in the moment. Being a champion implies that you are looking to the future.

If I said "Think like a winner," and you lost, how would you feel? Like a winner? I don't think so. On the other hand, if I said "Think like a champion," and you lost, how would you feel? Oh, you might still feel defeated, but your focus would change from the present to the future.

This isn't an exercise in semantics, but there's a shift in your *meme*. What is a meme? A meme is an alteration in an apex. It is a new way of determining excellence. Once a meme replaces a standard, it becomes a new benchmark. This whole idea of being a champion is a meme. Lots of books advocate your being a winner. I like winners, and I like to win. Who doesn't? On the other hand, I think of myself as a champion because it's my personal meme. It's an advance to the next level. To build this champion ship, you must have a purpose, a purpose that drives you and pushes you toward new and better performance memes. This purpose cannot be your secret—it must be your passion.

Art Linkletter put it this way: "Do a little more than you are paid to do. Give a little more than you have to. Try a little harder than you want to. Aim a little higher than you think possible. Give a lot of thanks to God for health, family, and friends." To build a champion ship, you must love what you are doing. That's right. I said love. Why on earth would you spend a lifetime doing something you didn't love? Loving what you do shows commitment. Champions love the quest for getting better.

One of the most successful people I know failed at business several times in his life. He didn't give up, because he loved it. His champion ship finally carried him through to success. To build a champion ship, you must believe what you are doing. I've met some professionals who spent the majority of their adult lives preparing for work in which they have no interest. Education is not the key. Experience won't do it, and neither will advancement. The opportunity to excel, to be the best, to have fulfillment at your work, depends on your belief system. To sell a concept such as championship sometimes requires a little finesse. It's not a big thing. What makes a leader a leader is a combination of a lot of little things.

Do you know the difference between water at 211° F and the same water at 212° F? At 211° F it's just hot water. At 212° F, it boils. The difference in the prize money of the first-place horse at the Kentucky Derby and the second-place horse is enormous. Have you ever seen a horse win the Kentucky Derby by a lap? It's usually won by a nose. Most people see their jobs the way a mosquito sees a nudist camp: they see all kinds of opportunity, but they can't decide where to start.

George Burns was one of my favorite comedians. With so many people in the comedy business, how did he keep his edge? Listen to his advice: "Fall in love with what you are doing for a living. To be able to get out of bed and do what you love to do for the rest of the day is beyond words. I would rather be a failure in something that I love than to be successful in something that I hate." When he was asked about his longevity, he replied, "I'm having too much fun to leave." George Burns's big goal was to live to be 100 years old and to have a birthday party in Beverly Hills. He did both.

It makes you wonder why George was a short-term planner. My goal is to live to be 100 years old, buy a new home, finance it for 30 years, and pay it off. That's optimism. I wrote a little poem about the abilities of leaders being the essence of the champion ship. It goes like this:

Winners yearn for prizes won.
They are addicted to luster.
Champions work just as hard
With all that they can muster.
Winners, for the circle of honor,
Their prize of renown and rank,
Champions, for the prize of knowing
Competitors at their flank.
The prize is the very same,
So what is there to matter?
One's the prize that joys the heart,
The other's the joy to flatter.

As you build your champion ship, you'll encounter wins. On your way to success you will have setbacks and failures. These are facts of life. Champions see both wins and losses as tools they will use to become leaders.

Will these four transitions, or ships, that we've been discussing make a difference in your life? Will they automatically transform you into a new and better person? I think so. They may not be the answer, but they are one small number in the final tally of what a person's life is supposed to be.

When I think of these ships, I just imagine that when you are finished building them, you will find yourself the proud owner of a ship that will bring your personal, professional, and spiritual life closer to fulfillment. It's not easy! Remember the warning of the hobby shop clerk: "I sell a few of those ships in a bottle, but I doubt very seriously that many of them are put together. It takes too long." But it is well worth the effort!

15

Energize Your Standards

Analyzing the prize: So what's next?

Commit to the Lord whatever you do, and your plans will succeed.—PROVERBS **16:3.**

We will complete several exercises that are designed to help you analyze the next steps you need to take in becoming the prize. The first exercise requires you to put down this book and get a piece of paper. I want you to make a paper airplane. Go ahead! The amazing thing about your plane is that you can make it almost subconsciously, without thought, because you've done it a million times.

Now, as you fold your paper airplane I want you to take a look at it. Have you done this before? The answer is probably yes. Do you know what? If I asked you to do it again six months from now, chances are you'd make that paper airplane the same way.

In just a moment you are going to turn the page of this book. When you do, there's going to be a design for a *different* type of paper airplane. But before we get to that, you have to hear a story.

My travels often take me to one of those cities that you hate to love—Washington, D.C. I love the town, hate the traffic. Love the monuments, don't like the crowds. But no matter how many times I go there, there's always an activity in which I love to participate. I love to go to the Smithsonian Institution, specifically the National

Air and Space Museum. Maybe it's because I spent 22 years in the Air National Guard. Maybe it's because I'm fascinated with aircraft. Maybe it's just because I can stroll around these wonderful static displays and, for a moment, imagine how these people from the past felt—excited, ecstatic, but scared. Their creations were new. Nobody had ever before done what they did. They were firsts. That's why they are so intriguing.

On one of my visits to the Smithsonian I stumbled upon a contest, a paper airplane-making contest. Seven- and 8-year-old children from a local school had gathered to participate. The contest consisted of two parts. Part one was for the best-designed airplane. Part two was for the accuracy with which it flew. The child who designed the best paper airplane would win the prize.

On the floor in front of these 13 young children, about 15 feet away, was a large circle made out of tape. One by one the children stepped forward and gave their names, then threw their plane into the circle. What intrigued me was that each child's plane looked pretty much like everybody else's plane. All of them, that is, until Eddie's. Eddie was the last child, and he was a little different. I don't mean in the way he looked—he was a little shorter. No, Eddie was different because he was holding a *box* under his arm. All the other competitors held their planes in their hands, but Eddie's was concealed in the box.

He stepped forward and put his box down by his side. Then he looked around as if he made eye contact with every person in that room. He said, "The dream of every person on this planet is the dream to fly, to excel, to build upon the knowledge of the society before them." (Pretty amazing, huh?) Then he reached into his box and took out the plane.

Had you been there, you would have thought the same thing I did: *That's not a plane.* You see, the plane Eddie had made is the plane you will soon make. It doesn't look like a paper airplane, but it flies like one. Maybe it flies too much like one, maybe even better than we would expect a paper airplane to fly. It will do tricks. It's an amazing thing!

Paper airplane design had been changed by a small 8-year-old boy. Without intervention you would continue to make your airplane like you always have. The reason for this exercise is to teach you a new way to make a paper airplane, to teach you a new way of thinking. Eddie created for me a new meme, a new way of setting excellence, a new way of looking at my standard.

"TRINITY" PLANE

1. **Fold #1:** Fold an 8½" x 11" piece of paper one third the way on the long side.
2. **Fold #2:** Along the same edge as fold #1, fold another one third.
3. **Fold #3:** Along the same edge as fold #2, fold another one third. Note: folds #2 and #3 are along the same side of paper as fold #1.
4. With folds facing down, drag paper over the edge of a table.
5. Unfold fold #3.
6. Slide right edge of paper under all folds to form a cylinder.
7. Refold fold #3.

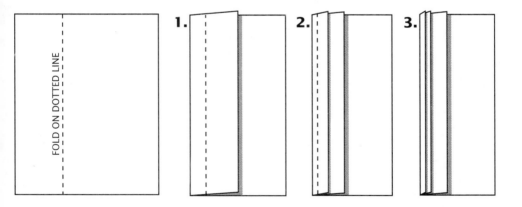

FOLD ON DOTTED LINE

When you are ready to fly your plane after its construction, there are two ways to do it: you can throw it like a football, with the weighted end to the front; or you can grasp it with your fingers inside the tube, and throw it straight up. It will do loop-the-loops and all types of interesting gyrations.

Most of us believe we can't be changed by a small, insignificant event. But not the prize—the prize knows that at any time in their life, at any moment, they not only *can* be changed but *will* be changed. In every interaction, in everything we do, we are changed.

For a moment let's think about an EKG, that throbbing, jumping line we see on medical shows that signifies life. Those spikes represent the electrical charge that the heart gives during its pumping. Imagine that your EKG, your meme of success—your standard—is flat-lining. What causes the standard to go up or down? Interaction with others and the choices you make as you travel around, regardless of the situation or the people you meet. Your EKG of success will either be improved or decayed, depending upon the people with whom you choose to associate. Some people will try to bring you down; others will try to accentuate your performance. Try your best to associate yourself with those who will improve your standard.

Before you can improve that standard, you must understand how it is manufactured. This will require another exercise. Unlike the paper plane exercise, this exercise will be done in your mind. I don't want any person outside of your own self to know what you are doing. I want no physical proof of the self-evaluation that you are getting ready to do. Let's begin.

Imagine that in front of you is a clean sheet of paper with no lines; it's perfectly blank. In your hand you have a pencil or a pen. On the top left-hand side of the sheet, number from one to five in your mind; then pick out an individual. This person will be your prize. Think about a person in your organization whom you admire—someone who gives good service, who values things of integrity, someone whose behavior you'd like to emulate. Have you got that person's face in your mind?

Good. On your imaginary sheet of paper, with your imaginary writing tool in your hand, write five characteristics of this person. Consider these gifts that they have, and, as you write them on your imaginary sheet of paper, burn them into your mind. What you are doing is creating a word picture of this person, describing the things at which they excel.

Now imagine someone in your organization or someone whom you know personally who is what I refer to as a personality vacuum. No matter what the situation, this person tends to cause your standard, your success EKG, to drop. This person isn't a bad person; he or she just doesn't know how to excel. On the right-hand side of your imaginary paper, number from one to five, and list five characteristics of this person. Consider them carefully.

What we have created on that sheet of white paper in your mind is a dichotomy. On the left you have five characteristics of an outstanding individual. A prize, you would call them. On the right you have five characteristics of a person who is definitely not a prize. We would call them the antiprize, a person who will stay in the box and be happy to be there.

Between these two lists of words I want you to draw a straight horizontal line connecting the two lists. Exactly in the center of that line, between these two lists of words, place a large dot.

It's evaluation time. Where do you fit on this line? (Oh, no! You can't pick the middle. God doesn't want us to be in the middle. He even tells us that to sit on the fence makes us worse than to be against Him.) Are you on the positive side of the dot, toward the prize but not exactly as far as you would like to be? Are you falling on the right-hand side of the dot, perhaps wishing that you could be on the positive side, wanting to move closer to the left?

If you honestly complete this exercise, you will fall within a minority of people in this country. This group is so small, so exclusive, that just by the completion of this exercise you will move to the left of the dot. At least you know where you fit. And now that you know, you can move.

Almost everyone will tell you that in every forum of self-diagnosis the pure admission of your weaknesses and the compilation of your strengths is one of the biggest decisions you will make. Before we leave this exercise, though, I would like you to do one more thing.

Go to the bottom of your imaginary sheet of paper and draw a line. On that line, put the name of the person you thought of for the left-hand side, for the positive things. Beneath that line, draw another line, and write your name there. Under your name, write the name of the person you thought of for the right-hand side.

Earlier in this book we talked about a three-step method of improvement. On the top step is a stretcher, a person who will make you better if you allow them to and if you emulate that person's behavior. On that middle step will be you. And on that bottom step is someone you can help, not by giving them advice, but by modeling for them.

This exercise was designed for two reasons. One, to help you understand where you are in the process of becoming the prize. Two, to make you better through allowing you to become the teacher. Our values are we ourselves. Without much conscious thought we tend to let others see these values as they watch us each day. Through watching us, they are changed either for the good or for the bad. You see, their straight line is affected by us, just as our line is affected by them. I want the exchange of influence to be such a positive one that you and the mentoree have a positive experience.

For our next exercise I'd like you to examine the list of personal values on the following page. Many of us think we have values, but we do not. Many of us see the values we have in life accurately, but we don't know how to make them better. That's why we're going to do this exercise. From this list of personal values, select five of them. Try not to rank them in any particular order; simply pick out your top five. After you choose your top five personal values, I want to show you, through a story, how easily our values can be taken away from us.

★ ★ ★

Let's imagine that you have won a prize. You get to fly around the world free of charge. You're going to be given $50,000 so you can really enjoy your two-week vacation. You are on the plane, comfortably seated in your first-class seat, enjoying all the amenities that service can afford.

Values Clarification

Not everything can be equally important. Decisions require awareness of priorities for resolving conflicts. This exercise will help you set priorities among your personal values.

PERSONAL VALUES

ACHIEVEMENT (sense of accomplishment, masterly)

ADVANCEMENT (promotion)

ADVENTURE (new and challenging experiences)

AFFECTION (love, caring)

COMPETITIVENESS (winning, taking risks)

COOPERATION (working well with others, teamwork)

CREATIVITY (being imaginative, innovative)

ECONOMIC SECURITY (steady, adequate income)

FAME (being famous, well known)

FAMILY HAPPINESS

FREEDOM (independence, autonomy)

FRIENDSHIP (close relationships with others)

HEALTH (being physically and mentally well)

HELPFULNESS (assisting others, improving society)

INNER HARMONY (being at peace with yourself)

INTEGRITY (honesty, sincerity, standing up for beliefs)

INVOLVEMENT (participating with others, belonging)

LOYALTY (duty, respectfulness, obedience)

ORDER (tranquillity, stability, conformity)

PERSONAL DEVELOPMENT (use of potential)

PLEASURE (fun, laughs, leasurely lifestyle)

POWER (control, authority, influence over others)

RECOGNITION (respect from others, status)

RELIGION (strong religious beliefs, closeness to God)

RESPONSIBILITY (accountable for results)

SELF-RESPECT (pride, sense of personal identity)

WEALTH (making money, getting rich)

WISDOM (understanding life, discovering knowledge)

All of a sudden the plane begins to shake. The pilot comes on and informs you that all power in the plane is gone and that the plane will crash. Unfortunately, there aren't enough parachutes to go around, but you can have one if you give up one of your values. (At this point I want you to cross out the value you would give up. Think carefully! Which value won't you need during this point in your life?)

You are safely on the ground. Unfortunately, you're in the middle of the deepest, darkest part of Africa. You have no idea how to get out. You have no way of protecting yourself. You have no shelter. You have the clothes on your back and the shoes on your feet. You don't even have a shaving kit or cosmetics.

This situation might be almost as bad as the one you just came from were it not for a person who is willing to take you to civilization. But since your money, credit cards, and belongings are now lying somewhere in the jungle, you have no way of paying this person to take you to safety. However, you decide to give up another of your values. (Consider the matter carefully, and cross one out. It's a value you will not need in this situation, and will give up.)

You next find yourself on the coast. No one knows you, and you have to get home. There's a steamer that will take you home across the ocean, but with no money and no way of paying for your trip . . . That's right! You must give up one of your values. (Consider carefully, and cross one out.)

You are almost home now. You can look off the bow of the ship and see the U. S. coastline, and you feel comfortable. Then you get the news that your ship is sinking. By now I'm sure you've guessed what you must do to get a life preserver. You must give up a value. It's going to be hard to give it up, you see. You've saved the last two. Probably the two that were most important. Although I asked you not to rate them, I'm sure you've saved the two that you liked most up to this point in the exercise. Consider it carefully, and cross one out.

You are home now with those you love, talking about your

adventure, clinging to your last remaining value. What is it? What thing did you hold on to so strongly; what means more to you than anything else? What personal value have you chosen? It's the starting point. What you have before you, the value you have before you, is a gem. It is a medal greatly prized and most precious. But it is a starting point.

None of the values that you chose from are really any stronger or any weaker than the others. I would hope that some of those that you have chosen included your faith, the choice to keep a strong religious belief and closeness to God, because, in reality, He is the most powerful of our values. With the help of God you will get home.

We must understand the process of becoming the prize. To be the prize, we must prioritize the challenges before us in order to build our confidence. We must understand, through this prioritization, that a positive attitude between ourselves and those we lead and with those whom we work will cause us to clean them up. We have to recognize that those people have desires and needs, and they have to be individualized through the help that we give them and through our involvement.

We have to have a vision, a vision with which to zing those with whom we work with service and with a positive attitude. Through this system of becoming the prize we will be energized to do the process again. The prize is so important, yet so misunderstood.

As we come to the end of our time together I want to tell you how honored I am that you went on this journey with me. Now I'd like to ask you to read the following short passage:

"Won supporter dime wonder fodder overcoat three washer ladle buoy heroes wall king on us pompous prom witty widow ratchet. Andy flounder chair retreat end widow ratchet end chapter down. Dentist popper campus trolling buy.

"'Husband hopping dun much hairy treat?' set he.

"'Doughnut must a gut,' saddest sun Gorge. 'I con a toll ally. Idea nitwit ma widow ratchet.'

"Den is fodder loss distemper and tick a swish unpadded ladle judge tillers can was soar."

Here is a one-question test: Whom is the passage about?

Read the passage again. Maybe you didn't understand it. Whom are we talking about here? You have no clue. Well, go somewhere private and read the passage aloud as quickly as you are able. Read it with a rhythm, and then see if you can answer the question. I know you can, because what you have done is to use another modality. You not only read it, you listened.

To say that you read this book would delight me very much. But to say that you *got* it would give me ultimate joy. Not because of some idea I have, but because you took action. You are well on your way to becoming the prize.

Congratulations!